'there'—throughout the exciting birth and growth of Trinidad and Tobago's distinguished badge of indigenous accomplishment, the **National Commercial Bank**—he is able to show us gently and modestly how much the 'revolution' that was NCB is so much the evolution of ourselves.

All well written, all well appreciated.

Alfred Aguiton
Chairman and Managing Director
All Media Projects Limited

===

REVIEW

About the Author and Book

The author was first exposed to the elements of banking from the perspective of Banking as a "Regulator." His entry into the Central Bank wherein he worked as Corporate Secretary exposed him to a wide and varied range of information, thus benefitting him with an endowment of knowledge availed principally through his "inquisitive mind."

In his quest for greater knowledge and getting things done, research then became natural for the man Philip G. Rochford – (PG or PGR.) His ascension into the foray of the Commercial Banking sector as the first "home grown" local banker and Chief Executive allowed him to chart a definitive course for indigenous commercial banking operations in Trinidad and Tobago, while facilitating the Eric Williams led government Policy Prescriptions to follow with the localization of Banks with Foreign ownership as well as for "Localization" of enterprises of various types of industry.

While the author started off as Manager of the Bank's first Unit, as the rapid expansion of NCB progressed, Philip (PG) was to be made Managing Director, then advanced with yet another first as Chairman and Managing Director thus becoming the "envy" of his counterparts within the non-indigenous Banking arena.

In changing the manner of the conduct of banking in Trinidad and Tobago so significantly, PG paved the way and facilitated an explosion of the housing stock. This was achieved as the NCB embarked upon a unique initiative in providing mortgage loans for housing and land loans for house construction with 90% financing on extremely favorable terms and conditions, and in areas or locations hitherto not provided.

Simultaneously the author - PG set about strategically to re-balance gender neglect in financial matters and career aspirations, as NCB launched a marketing campaign dubbed "Putting the Spotlight on Women." Women were to benefit for the first time in the history of banking in Trinidad and Tobago from equality of treatment in borrowing for home acquisition mortgages, jointly with their husbands or indeed singly. "Lifting the bar" much higher several female employees became the beneficiaries of management positions within NCB – a first in the industry.

Clearly then as "the Economist in PG" can affirm, NCB became a major force in facilitating the growth of the housing stock and the expansion of the economy. It is on record as well as acceptable economic theory that construction and infrastructure development have always been deemed to be a key driver of economic activities not only in Trinidad and Tobago, but globally. So that when you move around and look at the housing stock, note that PG and his well-trained cadre of professional staff must be credited.

ALSO BY PHILIP GUY ROCHFORD, HBM

B.Sc. (Econ.), M.Sc.(Accounting),
Chartered Accountant, FCIB, ACIS,
Reiki Master/Teacher, Certified Mediator
QSCA Law of Attraction Certified Coach

Live a Life of "Virtual" Success,

The Executive Speaks, Infinite Possibilities,

Glimpses of Greatness, Reflective Empowerment,

From Humble Beginnings
(Biography of Dr. Anthony Norman Sabga)

Enlightened Corporate Leadership,

Think, Be Still & Grow Spiritually,

10 Proven 21ˢᵗ Century Success Generators

Co-author of the Bestseller Wake Up...Live the Life You Love:
A Search for Purpose, compiled by Steven E and Lee Beard

Co-author of *Discover Your Inner Strength,*
Interviewer: David E. Wright
Published by Insight Publishing

Co-author of *No Winner Ever Got There Without a COACH*
Interviewer: David E. Wright
Published by Insight Publishing.

In Reader Views Literary Awards, *Reflective Empowerment* was selected as the "Walsh Seminars Award for Best Personal Growth Book of the Year (2010).

BOOK REVIEWS OF "NATIONAL COMMERCIAL BANKING IN TRINIDD AND TOBAGO"

A Positive Step In Consciousness

REVIEW

1. Philip Rochford's book on national commercial banking is much more than a history of the entity known as the National Commercial Bank (**'NCB'**) from its inception in 1970 to the time of its merger as the primary institution in the entity which became known as First Citizens Bank (**'FCB'**) in September, 1993. The book not only touches in part on the social economic history of Trinidad and Tobago, but also deals with the template of a set of policies which could be used to assist in the successful launch of new enterprises.

2. The book is written by a person who was at the forefront of all the major developments in indigenous banking in Trinidad and Tobago over a period of 23 years and the story is told in a measured and unemotional fashion. It is recommended reading for those who are interested in the development of indigenous banking, socio economic history of Trinidad and Tobago at the time that the NCB was launched, and the circumstances and events leading to the birth of FCB.

3. We live in a society and world where fact becomes obscured by rumor, distortion and misinformation. Those who purport to pronounce in a flippant and authoritative manner at the same time on issues covered

by the book will do well to consult its contents before speaking.

4. For the younger generation who have been fortunate to attain the age of majority in an era where discrimination on the grounds of color and ethnicity has been significantly eliminated, it should be an education for them to learn that discrimination did exist in the banking industry in a substantial fashion around 1970 as documented in the report of the late Professor Lloyd Braithwaite. It is recommended reading for such individuals.

5. One theme which attracted my attention as a corporate lawyer was the controversy surrounding the appointment of the late Mr Frank Rampersad and Mr Samuel Martin who at the time were government employees. They were nominated to the Board of the NCB by the Minister of Finance. Such a move was regarded as setting up a situation where political interference would occur in the affairs of the NCB and there was criticism in the media.

6. Having served as a director of the NCB for a 4 year period between 1989-1993, it was my experience that there was never the slightest suggestion of political interference at the level of the board. However, sadly we live in a society where that is not the case in a number of state enterprises. Our culture is one which encourages or accepts that persons nominated by a Minister to sit on a Board would act in accordance with the wishes (real or imaginary) of his/her appointer. This **'yes man'** syndrome which has been condemned by judges in the common law world is an unfortunate part of the local corporate culture which suggests that a nominated director is somehow incapable of exercising independent judgment.

7. Another feature of the book which attracted my attraction was that the author was one of the persons who had the foresight to initiate and be part of the process which culminated in the merger of the NCB with the Cooperative Bank and the Workers' Bank in 1993. Without fear for losing his personal position (as happens in the case of many mergers in the corporate world), he played a significant role in the initial steps towards the merger and then went into retirement without recognition or rancor.

8. At the end of the day, I consider that Philip Rochford has made a significant contribution by placing on record the initial 23 year of significant indigenous commercial banking in Trinidad and Tobago. It is hoped that his contribution will be recognised in this part of the world which is not known to be generous with magnanimity.

Claude H. Denbow S.C.
Dr. Claude H. Denbow, S.C.
Attorney-at-Law

===

REVIEW

Once again, **Author Philip Guy Rochford** makes history readable, revisiting the past to plumb the prologue that it is, extracting the relevant illumination, joy and wisdom so very useful to guide the future.

Rochford—in this book, he's the ex-banker and financial guru—gives facts and figures their appropriate humane and historic contexts.

Moreover, having been the influencer who was actually

Examples of the explosion of the housing stock can be found in "every corner" of Trinidad and Tobago, but in particular South Trinidad and along the East/West corridor. One such notable development is the then Neal and Massy/Matalon infused Santa Rosa pre-fabricated housing development, whose private sector construction **was financed in part** by the National Commercial Bank (NCB) and the long term mortgages to individual borrowers provided by the NCB Trust Company for up to 25% of the total number of housing Units. Prudent banking in managing risks dictated that limited level of mortgage lending in a single project.

The visionary leadership of the author in using the Bank as a driver for economic development was boundless. It never stopped and not limited to home ownership nor consumer loans. The Park and Henry Street Branch was home to two of the largest commercial loans providing Financing to upwards of sixty-five million dollars thirty and thirty-five million respectively, for the construction of Plants on the Point Lisas Industrial Estate in Couva, Trinidad.

One of his - PG's Visions was building out of significant infrastructure for housing its expanded network of Bank branches, with the added value of simultaneously generating employment opportunities in all sectors including, but not limited to areas of hardware sales, trucking and skills training among others. National Commercial Bank built one of the longest buildings with extensive floor area spanning a full block from Abercromby Street on the East to St. Vincent Street on the West in Port of Spain in which was housed the operations of two of its Subsidiaries, NCB Trust Company and TRINFINANCE, as well as an NCB Bank Branch, known as the St. Vincent Street Branch.

Another one of its then new construction is that iconic and

now historic building, which through PG's foresight became the home of the Bank's Head Office and a Bank Branch at the corner of Park and Henry Streets. That Park Street structure simulating and complementing the neighboring Rosary R.C Church was formally opened by the founding father of the Nation, Dr. the Right Honorable Eric Williams in 1977. These two uniquely designed buildings were designed by architects normally not used by the international banks.

PG in this book demonstrated how much of a discerning eye he had for Human Resources – training and development. Several Managers therefore were exposed to and became beneficiaries of structured programs in commercial banking at Overseas Banks, notably National Westminster Bank in London England.

The establishment of a Training Center in the then central district of Chaguanas further facilitated upgrading employees' skills. Chaguanas later became the Borough of Chaguanas, then housing the most modern Training Center in the English Speaking Caribbean, established by the National Commercial Bank.

By the time of retirement of the first Chief Executive, twenty-three years after the bank started, it is reported that there were more than eighty people with tertiary level education in such fields as banking, accounting, information technology, law, administration, financing, and human resources—a figure that far outdistanced the staff make-up in any of the other banks in Trinidad and Tobago. Moreover, a number of employees trained at the National Commercial Bank eventually migrated to senior positions elsewhere in the Corporate world.

In closing this review of the author's book –"National Commercial Banking in Trinidad and Tobago", sub-titled A Positive Step in Consciousness, it must be said that there is a body of views, which notwithstanding the best efforts of the NCB, its Board and Management, that much more could have been done for financial nurturing of those within the Diaspora, who indeed were in the majority within the NCB's customer base. Initiatives could have been pursued for "Business Incubator - type arrangements" to chart a course for successful transformation of the younger group of 'at risk' entrepreneurs into an "Elite group" of business people derived from within this "indigenous grouping".

Such an innovation - an Incubator Division operated within the NCB Trust Company may have spawned further growth and development and perhaps financial independence of more individuals and businesses than might be generally known, while saving others "from falling over the cliff," or from experiencing personal loss or business failures.

An example of such an initiative to grow financial strength and minimize financial loss or failures, which is not narrated by the author can be found during the period of Hon. A.N.R Robinson's Government of the National Alliance for Reconstruction (NAR), when salaries of public servants and some State Enterprises including employees at NCB were cut by 10% leading to reduced cash flows of employees and loan and mortgage delinquencies within the customer base of the NCB Trust Company.

In response to this situation, it was amazing to witness a project at NCB Trust Company (a wholly owned subsidiary of NCB) that provided financial counseling to persons with house mortgage arrears, resulting from the economic meltdown in Trinidad and Tobago at that time. Some thirty young graduates of the University of the West Indies staffed what can be described as a "Personal Specialist Incubator"

The intention was to ensure the protection of many mortgagors' homes from sales on the "auction block." Marriages too were also saved through financial counseling and social guidance, while the education of children of mortgagors were protected and not compromised during those memorable days; thus, overall the fabric of many families were saved from social or financial distress.

One of the spin-offs of this incubator project was that the training and experience gained by the specialist counselors of the Unit facilitated their subsequent employment in high offices in such organizations as the Central Bank, the Office of the Director of Public Prosecution, The Judiciary – Supreme Court of Trinidad and Tobago, as well as the International Criminal Court based in the Hague. Two of them became Judges of the Supreme Court, while one became a Judge of the International Criminal Court. So far reaching was the Vision for a local Commercial Bank, and opportunities created firstly by Dr. the Honorable Eric Eustace Williams, the first Prime Minister of the then eight year old Independent Nation of Trinidad and Tobago and very well executed by that innovative guy – Philip Guy Rochford, the first Manager of the NCB, the first Managing Director and the first Executive Chairman of the Bank.

Phillip Guy Rochford is a visionary, a coach, an inspirational leader and a mentor, who recognized talent quickly and used it wisely in the interest of the whole Organization. As a recipient of his counsel from 1975 when he facilitated my employment at NCB after I boldly applied for a JOB for which there was no "advertised position or vacancy," I can truly affirm that it was an inherent open-mindedness, which allowed PG to craft a TEMPLATE for establishing and developing a business in a matured competitive industry to be formulated. Such a template can be equally applied as a guide by new and existing businesses to grow successfully as they conduct their businesses within the different markets.

One of the main objectives of this book is seeking to provide an initial set of policies that can deepen the strategies to assist in the successful launch and development of new enterprises seeking to enter an established competitive matured industry. While telling the true story of the National Commercial Bank, readers will find within this book that the author has surpassed the expectations. On-going and even more mature enterprises can be beneficiaries as well.

I commend the author for this historical contribution and forward thinking of the business of indigenous Banking and the National Commercial BANK – NCB, an Institution not borne too soon. I encourage Managers and senior Executives from all industries to read, study and embrace the contents of this book – "National Commercial Banking in Trinidad and Tobago ... A Positive Step In Consciousness."

As you read I invite you to take on board of course the contents of the extensive list of nineteen items of the TEMPLATE for successful entrepreneurship, five of the major PILLARS serving as the foundation to a successful enterprise, as well as the special note on that which I shall call the "PITFALLS", but which PG in this book has labelled as 'The FIVE FINANCIAL TRAPS.' The lessons presented must be useful to both existing and new entrepreneurs.

Arnold Piggott
Chairman, Education Facilities Company Limited [EFCL]
(Former Manager of NCB Trust Company Limited
&Former Corporate Manager of NCB)
(Former Cabinet Minister of the Government of
Trinidad and Tobago)

==================================

NATIONAL COMMERCIAL
BANKING
IN TRINIDAD AND TOBAGO
A POSITIVE STEP IN CONSCIOUSNESS

PHILIP GUY ROCHFORD

Former Chairman & Managing Director
of National Commercial Bank of Trinidad and Tobago Limited

Foreword by Eden Shand, Environmentalist,
Author of "The Estates Within": A docu-drama,
Former Minister in the National Alliance for
Re–construction (NAR) Government of Trinidad and Tobago

BALBOA.
PRESS
A DIVISION OF HAY HOUSE

Scripture quotations marked KJV are from the Holy Bible, King James Version (Authorized Version). First published in 1611. Quoted from the KJV Classic Reference Bible, Copyright © 1983 by The Zondervan Corporation.

Author's photograph by Ms. Alison Punch of Fotocraft Limited. (Trinidad and Tobago)

Logo three circle design with arrow on front book cover by All Media Projects Limited (Trinidad and Tobago)

All excerpts from Annual Reports of National Commercial Bank of Trinidad and Tobago Limited (NCB) by courtesy of Mr. Philip Guy Rochford, Former Chairman and Managing Director of NCB

Balboa Press books may be ordered through booksellers or by contacting:

Balboa Press
A Division of Hay House
1663 Liberty Drive
Bloomington, IN 47403
www.balboapress.com
1 (877) 407-4847

Print information available on the last page.

ISBN: 978-1-5043-7916-8 (sc)
ISBN: 978-1-5043-7918-2 (hc)
ISBN: 978-1-5043-7917-5 (e)

Library of Congress Control Number: 2017906638

Balboa Press rev. date:05/01/2017

CONTENTS

FOREWORD

FOREWORD BY MR. EDEN SHAND

Philip Guy Rochford is best known for his midwifery at the birth of the National Commercial Bank of Trinidad and Tobago (NCB) and for his leadership of this enterprise for almost a quarter of a century. And yet, in spite of his prolific retirement authorship of multiple books, he has steered clear of writing about this fascinating and intriguing subject. We are grateful to his wife, who has finally persuaded him to tell the true story of the NCB.

The closure of the NCB and the takeover of its business by a larger newly-formed State enterprise, First Citizens Bank, coincided with the mandatory retirement of Rochford. In some quarters, the NCB was made to look like a failure, but Rochford held his tongue as he eschewed self-defense. In writing the true story, he had the ideal opportunity to set the record straight, but readers with a penchant for bacchanal would be sadly disappointed. He has pointed fingers at no one, but has dwelled on the positivity of the story.

Rochford, without a doubt, is a most positive person. His book is entitled *National Commercial Banking in Trinidad and Tobago,* but he has appended a seemingly puzzling sub-title *A Positive Step in Consciousness.* Therein, his positivity is evident, but what is the connection between banking history and consciousness? It is only when one arrives at the last chapter, *Moral of the Banking Story.* that, beyond positivity, one catches a glimpse of his spirituality, more fully discerned in all of his previous books. Rochford has written his book, not merely to shift the needle positively in the quest to improve commercial banking activities, but as a step in raising consciousness of Society.

The Society of Trinidad and Tobago is largely unconscious – spiritually, environmentally, economically – and much needs to be done by leaders like Rochford to raise this consciousness. He has most certainly done so in the vital area of national banking. Undoubtedly, NCB was a success, notwithstanding the questionable low valuation of its shares, and the secrets of this success in the many areas – philosophy, communications, product development, operations, human resource development, community outreach - have been detailed in the book, which he could not have divulged while he was Chairman and Managing Director of NCB. The book is chocked full of information on how to succeed in business, not only in banking, but in any sector where an enthusiastic, though inexperienced, entrant might face established competition.

In his retirement, Rochford has become a qualified Life Coach and he has plunged into this calling with the same dedication that he had for the development of national banking. It is not surprising, therefore, to find him donning his coach's hat in the last chapter of his book, written in the first person, to present his personal testimony of what the NCB experience. meant to him. And he has translated the moral of his story into the exhortation to the reader to courageously follow one's dream so that one can be the best expression of oneself. Thereby, the collective consciousness of all like-minded readers will make for a prosperous Trinidad and Tobago.

This book is as timely as it is necessary. It is timely, as all octogenarian writing is. It is necessary because the population needs it. As the indigenous pioneer of national banking, Rochford has arrived at the fulfillment of a lifelong dream and is leaving behind a priceless legacy to the entrepreneurial posterity of Trinidad and Tobago.

EDEN SHAND
Mr. Eden Shand, Environmentalist,
Author of "The Estates Within": A Docu-drama,

DEDICATION

This work is dedicated to Trinidad and Tobago's POSTERITY. It is the story of men and women who had the courage and belief in themselves that the indigenous people of Trinidad and Tobago can successfully manage the critical resources of Trinidad and Tobago.

ACKNOWLEDGMENTS

Initiators: Dr. The Honorable Eric Eustace Williams, first Prime Minister of Trinidad and Tobago used his sense of history and keen vision to grasp the opportunity to establish the National Commercial Bank of Trinidad and Tobago Limited, through the acquisition of the Trinidad operations of the Bank of London and Montreal (BOLAM). During his lifetime he insisted that there would be no political interference in the operations of the Bank, and this is further cause for honoring Dr. Williams.

Mr. Dodderidge Alleyne, Permanent Secretary to the Prime Minister, and his negotiating team must be complimented for completing masterly negotiations for the acquisition of BOLAM.

Dr. Agathon Aerni, Swiss Advisor Banking Expert, convinced the Government of Trinidad and Tobago, to establish initially a Board of Directors free and independent of political affiliation, and Dr. Agathon Aerni must be fully acclaimed for this insight.

Mr. Karl Hudson-Phillips, Q.C., then Attorney General of the Government, is owed a special debt of gratitude for fashioning the Memorandum and Articles of Association of the Bank.

Board of Directors: Special acknowledgment must be given to the original members of the Board of Directors, and subsequent Directors who further strengthened the corporate governance of the Bank. The Directors' loyalty, independence, competence, and intensity provided the foundation for NCB's success.

Foreword: Mr Eden Shand, like so many others had his own obligations to fulfill, and thus I am truly grateful for the dedicated time he used to write the foreword. Eden in the 1970s, 1980s, and 1990s was one of the thought leaders in Trinidad and Tobago. He brought his usual insight and universal mind to commenting on, as well as analyzing the manuscript.

Reviewers: All the reviewers are to be congratulated for the great care and attention they displayed in reviewing the manuscript. **Dr. Claude Denbow, S.C.** was masterful in carefully analyzing the manuscript from his professional legal expertise, as well as his being a Director of National Commercial Bank for four tears. **Mr. Alfred Aguiton** is the Co-founder and Chairman of All Media Projects

Limited. He was connected with the advertising and public relations of National Commercial Bank, almost from its inception, and therefore is in a special position to assess the manuscript of the record of the journey of NCB.

Mr. Arnold Piggott held critical positions at the National Commercial Bank, such as Manager of the largest Branch at Independence Square, Manager of the NCB Trust Company, Manager of the Park & Henry Streets NCB Branch and Executive Assistant to the Managing Director. Thus, he had a deep and keen insight into the operations of NCB.

Mr. Nazeer Sultan had the good fortune to work as a Senior Manager for fifteen years at NCB, and twelve years at First Citizens Bank. He was one of two or three employees with this dual length of experience of both banks. Nazeer's review was so comprehensive and chronological that his review was included as an Epilogue. My undying thanks to all the reviewers for their care and attention to reading and assessing the manuscript.

Staff: My special thanks to the initial thirty-four members of staff who were recruited from the predecessor Bank of London and Montreal

(BOLAM). They were the foundation of the Bank and many of them rose to managerial positions within NCB. During the twenty-three years of the life of National Commercial Bank, over 2,000 persons were employed. Each one in his or her unique way contributed to the tapestry of the bank's success. I offer my special thanks to all of them. Some employees have been mentioned by name in the book, but this does not mean that the others did not make sterling contributions. It would have been cumbersome to mention individually all the 2,000 employees.

Customers: An organization exists to meet the needs of its customers. The growth of NCB'S customers from 18,000 customers to over 200,000 customers is a tribute that customers appreciated the Bank's efforts to delight them. Without the unstinting support of the customers the Bank would not have succeeded.

General Community: Apart from its customers, the Bank could not exist, unless it had the support of the general community. The Bank had its community outreach and the community responded positively. The general community must be complimented for supporting indigenous banking.

Supply Providers: The Bank needed to engage competent supply providers to effect its mandate. Architects, contractors, information technologists, attorneys-at-law, office suppliers and a host of other operatives made their services available to the Bank. Without these supply providers the Bank could not move forward, and thus the Bank's gratitude is in order. Mr. Henri Telfer provided the creative designs for the Annual Published Reports of NCB. Although Mr. Telfer was personally congratulated many times during his lifetime, I consider it important to record his contribution for posterity.

Family: My mother, Mrs. Amy Cox Rochford, first female qualified Pharmacist in Trinidad and Tobago, is responsible for all that I have achieved in life. Her skillful nurturing of my formation was phenomenal. I am grateful for my father who died when I was two years old, but he provided my DNA and generational culture base.

Without the unselfish support of my family during the journey of the Bank, its growth and success would not have been possible. I acknowledge their patience and understanding. One of the consequences of developing the Bank was that I was not always available to nurture my six children, as fully as

I considered appropriate. However, my delight is that I gave them their own voices, although I do not always agree with their voices.

Since my retirement from the Bank, my wife, Edlin, herself an author, has encouraged and actively supported me in telling the true story of National Commercial Bank, and I publicly thank her for this support.

INTRODUCTION

A life worth living is a life worth reviewing; this also applies to your career. From age thirty-seven to age sixty (i.e. twenty-three years) the author was Chief Executive of the National Commercial Bank of Trinidad and Tobago Limited. Also, a similar period of twenty-three years has passed since his retirement from the NCB, and thus it is an opportune time to review the author's banking career.

In July 1970 when the National Commercial Bank of Trinidad and Tobago Limited was established, there was no local template to guide its development. There were no guidelines established in Trinidad and Tobago to assist prospective entrepreneurs who wanted to start a local business in a competitive industry that had been in operation for many years.

This book serves to provide an initial set of policies that can deepen the strategies to assist in the successful launch and development of new enterprises seeking to enter an established competitive matured industry. Also, the contents of the book tell the actual story of commercial banking in Trinidad and Tobago. Some aspects of the operations of the National Commercial Bank are revealed herein.

A Prospective Template

Based on the experience of the journey of the National Commercial Bank of Trinidad and Tobago, a prospective Template, The Business Growth Template, for establishing and developing a business in a matured competitive industry can be formulated as follows:

(1) Establishment of a mission, and a strategic direction and plan.
(2) The need for branding the business.
(3) Assessing the nature, strengths, and weaknesses of the main competitors.
(4) Selecting customer delight as a very high priority.
(5) Identifying and providing products and services for which there is an effective demand, but the prevailing market does not provide them.
(6) Implementation of systems to deliver operational efficiency, including the internal audit function.
(7) Competitive terms and conditions of employment.
(8) Engender cohesiveness in the Board of Directors.
(9) Develop a strong executive management team.

(10) A Communication Framework for stakeholders

(11) Cultivating an atmosphere of mutual respect between management and other staff.

(12) Keeping abreast of technological advances in the industry.

(13) Establish clear corporate values.

(14) Ensure that the business is seen as a responsible Corporate Citizen.

(15) Generate sufficient residual income to sustain and grow the business.

(16) Craft a vigorous human resource policy, including training and discipline.

(17) Implement a Productivity Outreach.

(18) Defining the accountabilities for and responsibilities of the critical elements of the business

(19) Opportunities for career development

Firms are at different stages of development. Some will be in business already, some may be in expansion mode, and others may be in the conceptual stage. Thus, appropriate adaptations have to be made to cater for the emergence of particular parameters affecting different situations. Also, the sequencing of these nineteen elements of the Template will be determined by individual preferences.

Commercial Banking Story

The initial philosophy and implications of the journey of National Commercial Banking in Trinidad and Tobago are outlined. By the end of twenty-three years of the formal experiment, National Commercial Bank of Trinidad and Tobago Limited (NCB) had increased its market share from one percent to twelve percent, its branches from one to eighteen, its staff from thirty-five to 1800, established three subsidiaries and developed a cadre of financial managers who subsequently gained senior managerial positions in other financial institutions in Trinidad and Tobago and the wider Caribbean Region. Moreover, in each of its first twenty-two years of operations, it generated and publicly declared profits.

The challenges were that (a) there was no significant history of indigenous management of commercial banks and other financial institutions (b) there were seven international banks operating successfully in Trinidad and Tobago with a total of over 100 branches and (c) the Government of Trinidad and Tobago initially had 100% of the shareholding of NCB, and this weakened the public's confidence in the institution.

Necessity

What was the necessity for this preoccupation with indigenous banking when, at that time, with only about one million people in Trinidad and Tobago, there were already seven international accredited banks operating in the Country?

Trinidad and Tobago had been granted Political Independence by the United Kingdom in August 1962 but there was a general feeling by the population of Trinidad and Tobago that without Financial Independence, Independence was not complete. There was a strong public perception that the banking needs, and aspirations of the population were not being properly served by the international banks. This view was so widely held that the Government appointed a Commission of Enquiry into the racial and color discrimination in the private sector of Trinidad and Tobago, with particular reference to Banks and other Financial Institutions and matters therewith. The Commission was chaired by Professor Lloyd Braithwaite, a renowned Sociologist and then Principal of the St. Augustine Campus of the University of the West Indies. Terms of Reference of the Commission were as follows;

"By the powers vested in him under Section 2 of the Commissions of Enquiry Ordinance, Ch. 7, No. 2, His Excellency Sir Solomon Hochoy. G.C.M.G., G.C.V.O., O.B.E., deemed it advisable that an enquiry be held into *the incidence of racial and color discrimination in the private sector of the economy of Trinidad and Tobago with particular reference to Banks and other Financial Institutions and matters therewith,* and on 12th August 1969, appointed as Commissioners for such an enquiry:—

LLOYD BRAITHWAITE, ESQUIRE, B.A.
THE REVEREND BOYD REID
MRS. ESMEE OTTLEY
DR. MARTIN SAMPATH
ALDWYN POON TIP, ESQUIRE

DR. MICHAEL ALLEYNE
Secretary to the Commission"

The Commission submitted on 5th October 1970, an Interim Report that dealt with the Banks and other Financial Institutions. The basic conclusion was that there was racial and color discrimination in Banks and other Financial Institutions. The Commission's recommendations included:

- Establishment of a Race Relations Board
- Institution of a Public Education Program to combat the historical vestiges of racial and color inferiority
- Training through the establishment of a Banking Institute
- Launching of a Research Program in the field of race relations
- Introduction of Legislation to make discrimination in employment on grounds of race and color an offence; and administrative machinery be set up for its implementation
- Possibly in collaboration with the University of the West indies, set up an "Afro-Asian" or Caribbean Museum open to the general public in which the origins of the main racial groups and their background can be suitably displayed

Perspective of the Author's mandate

Commercial banking had been in existence in Trinidad and Tobago for very many years before National Commercial Bank (NCB) came into existence on 1st July 1970. The mandate for NCB was to provide improved banking services to the population of Trinidad and Tobago, and especially to impact areas that required improvement for the benefit of society.

Thus, in providing this account of NCB'S stewardship, the Author's focus was on what NCB did differently to the foreign banks, and not concentrate on products and services that were already provided by the other commercial banks.

The issue was to point to the positive distinction that NCB made through its operations. Moreover, the distinctions must be verifiable by a third party, and generally be evidenced by some public document at the time of the event.

Finally, no one individual was responsible for the success of NCB. The cumulative efforts of some 2,000 staff members who were employed over the 23-uear life span of NCB must be honored. All the names of the 2,000 employees have not been included in this historic account, but a number of them have been identified.

CHAPTER 1

HISTORY

Experience and training of the first Chief Executive of National Commercial Bank of Trinidad and Tobago Limited

It would be interesting and instructive, if a glimpse can be had into the formation and preparation of the person who was selected to lead the new charge for local commercial banking. This story is told in the words of Philip G. Rochford, the first Chief Executive of NCB. His personal narrative follows:-

"My interest in banking was aroused when I was pursuing my "A" level Economics of London University's examination, as a prelude to my following the path to become an Attorney-at-Law. There was a section, Money and Banking, in "A" level economics' syllabus, and I was not able to get help in this section from local scholars. In retrospect this was not surprising as there were no local commercial banks operating in Trinidad and Tobago and there were no citizens of the Country at the Head of any of the commercial banks or in very senior positions. At that time I gleaned that there was a growth opportunity in the commercial banking sector and I decided to pursue it.

"When I was awarded a Government Administrative Cadet Scholarship in 1960, Law was no longer offered for that scholarship, so I opted to pursue a degree in Economics, specializing in Money and Banking. Here I was in 1960, arriving in the "mother country" (a local familiar name for the United Kingdom), armed with a solid primary and secondary schooling, a firm family and community foundation, an always accompanying ambition to become a barrister—*and* a reality check for a scholarship to pursue money and banking.

Money and Banking

"The fates were once again intervening. I started off at the Oxford College of Technology, focused on the special subject option of money and banking. One year later, on instructions from the scholarship authorities in Trinidad, I was transferred to the University of Hull to study business economics. During my stay at Hull University, I completed the requirement to keep dining terms at Lincoln's Inn of Court.

"On the negative side of that first experience in England, I found myself being introduced to bigotry and racial discrimination. As an example, one of my next-door neighbors, who worked as a "char woman" serving tea, and whose husband was a worker on a scavenger truck, argued vehemently that she was better than any medical doctor who was black in color. Moreover, she said, "I'd never let a black doctor or black nurse touch me or attend to me.""

"Nor was my university free from expressions of overt superiority. I remember my senior economic history lecturer becoming very excited when he discovered that I was from Trinidad and Tobago. But he was not shy to share his considered opinion with me: "Your Dr. Eric Williams is a great historian, although he had it wrong with his thesis that slavery was abolished because of economic reasons and not for humanitarian reasons." The opinion generally held by European scholars at that time was that slavery was abolished because of humanitarian reasons. Dr. Williams established the counterpoint that slavery was abolished because the slavery plantation was no longer economically viable.

"Suffice it to say that with that stage of my tertiary first-world education completed, I said my thanks to all concerned and happily undertook the return trek home."

Some achievements of the National Commercial Bank (NCB)

There were many achievements of NCB during its life of twenty-three years from July 1970 to September 1993, and these will be indicated in the following pages. However, here are some indications to give a flavor of the overt and subtle accomplishments:

- Eliminated employment practices that discriminated on grounds of class, race, or location of applicant's address.
- Provided banking services to the neglected lower strata of society.
- Developed a professional cadre of local management to strengthen the banking system, as well as Corporate Trinidad and Tobago.
- Provided mortgage loans for housing and land loans for house construction on 90% financing terms, not previously available.
- Addressed female gender income discrimination where females were loan

applicants, or joint loan applicants for housing loans.

- Introduced banking and other initiatives that lifted the self-confidence and self-esteem of the Citizens of Trinidad and Tobago.
- Published profits for the first twenty-two years of NCB'S existence. Accounts for its twenty-third year, just prior to its merger into First Citizens Bank, are in contention.
- Increased the total deposits from $4.5 million in the first year in 1970 to over $1.5 billion in its final year in 1993.

CHAPTER 2

PHILOSOPHY OF NATIONAL COMMERCIAL BANKING

International Banks

Traditionally, in Trinidad and Tobago commercial banking was exclusively the province of international banks. There were at first the British institutions and later banks from the United States of America and Canada. By the turn of political independence in 1962, the semblance of indigenous banks were the Post Office Savings Bank and the Trinidad Co-operative Bank (familiarly called 'The Penny Bank'), but neither of the two was a commercial bank. However, both of these institutions paved the way for National Commercial Banking to be established.

The Post Office Savings Bank was Government owned. However, its operations were governed by an Act of Parliament, that vested the investment of deposits in the Crown Agents of Britain; also, there were no checking accounts that are associated with a commercial bank. However, there were many outlets in the outlying districts that gave persons throughout Trinidad and Tobago the facility to lodge their savings.

The Trinidad Co-operative Bank was neither a co-operative nor a bank. It was not operating under license as a Co-operative, or in possession of a commercial bank license. Nonetheless, this institution provided a platform for the citizenry, particularly the lower income group, to harness their savings. Trinidad Co-operative Bank was known as "The Penny Bank" and the Post Office Savings Bank had offices in rural and other places where the International Banks found the locations unprofitable.

Following Independence in 1962, the Government of Trinidad and Tobago moved to develop and strengthen local financial institutions. One aspect of this Government policy in 1969 was that bank licenses would be granted to a new foreign bank only if that bank intended to provide more than merely commercial banking services. There were already seven foreign banks with some one hundred branches in Trinidad and Tobago. Approval for new foreign bank licenses would be given for areas not then covered, such as merchant banking, leasing, and secondary mortgage financing. Need for National Commercial Banking as a local financial structure was integral to support Political Independence.

Thus, a further Government policy was introduced that new commercial bank branches would normally only be given to international banks which were incorporated locally; the requirement was that international banks had to be incorporated locally rather than merely being registered to do business in Trinidad and Tobago.

BIRTH OF THE NATIONAL COMMERCIAL BANK

In December 1969, a banker from Switzerland, Dr. Agathon Aerni, was carrying out an assignment for the Government of Trinidad and Tobago to establish an indigenous commercial bank. He was considering the feasibility of merging Trinidad Co-operative Bank and the Government-run Post Office Savings Bank. The difficulties included that Trinidad Co-operative Bank was neither a commercial bank nor a co-operative as defined by the governing legislation. The law restricted the Post Office Savings Bank in the use of its deposits.

Also, the majority of the Post Office locations were unsuitable for branches of a commercial bank by virtue of the physical state of their premises and security considerations.

While the positives and negatives of the merger between Trinidad Co-operative Bank and the Post Office Savings Bank were being assessed, an opportunity arose at the height of the 1970 Black Power Revolution—and some say *because of it*—for the Government of Trinidad and Tobago to acquire the Bank of London and Montreal (BOLAM).

BOLAM was owned by the Bank of Montreal, Barclays Bank, and the Bank of London and South America and maintained branches throughout Latin America. For some two years prior to 1970, the three banks were in negotiations to terminate the triumvirate ownership, and they eventually allocated each branch in the several countries to one of the three owners. In the case of Trinidad, BOLAM was allocated to Bank of Montreal. Barclays Bank in Trinidad (now Republic Bank) already had four branches within a half-mile radius of BOLAM and therefore was not interested in the Trinidad branch of BOLAM.

BOLAM issued a press release worldwide outlining the arrangements the owners had made and making it clear that the necessary licenses would have to be obtained from the Governments and Monetary Authorities of the various countries in which the banks were located. Before this event, the Government of Trinidad and Tobago had announced a policy decision that bank licenses would be granted to a new bank only if it intended to provide more than merely commercial banking. There were already seven foreign banks with some one hundred branches in Trinidad and Tobago.

Granting a license to a new foreign bank, the Bank of Montreal, was outside the established banking policy. The Government therefore moved to acquire the BOLAM branch in Trinidad, negotiating the transaction in quick time.

Mr. Philip G. Rochford, then Corporate Secretary of the Central Bank of Trinidad and Tobago, was offered the appointment of Chief Executive of the successor bank, the National Commercial Bank of Trinidad and Tobago Limited, and he accepted. **Thus, the mantle was placed upon him to be the Architect for positively shifting the National Commercial Banking paradigm. He accepted the challenge with humility, passion, and high expectations.**

Vision for National Commercial Banking

On 30th June 1970, in a broadcast to the Nation, Dr. The Right Hon. Eric Eustace Williams, Prime Minister of Trinidad and Tobago in a wide ranging address on National Reconstruction of the economy indicated that, the National Commercial Bank was one of the most important aspects of economic policy and programs involving the development of a larger network of financial institutions indigenous to Trinidad and Tobago. The main objective was mobilization of the capital resources required for the fulfillment of the development process and the channeling of those resources into those areas where they would best assist the national development effort.

Composition of the first Board of Directors of the bank was critical to engendering confidence within the public and to the bank being up to the task of managing the business. Mr. Cyril Duprey, Founder and Head of Colonial Life Insurance Company Limited, was appointed Chairman. Other directors were labor leader Mr. Vas Stanford, solicitor Mr. Norman Girwar, businessman Mr. Wilfred Lee Lum, co-operative movement official Mr. Ruthven Cheesman, Mr. Ewart Thorne, Queen's Counsel,

Mr. Sidney Knox, Chief Executive, Neal and Massy Holdings, Mr. Fitzroy Francis, economist and lecturer at the University of the West Indies, and Mr. Philip G. Rochford, Chief Executive of the National Commercial Bank. Thus, the board had representation from business, labor, law, academia, finance and central banking. There is no doubt that these original board members ensured that the bank was set on a success course, and through their solidarity NCB was able to resist any attempt at political interference in the operations of the bank.

Banking philosophy of NCB

NCB'S Philosophy

Although the test of profitability is probably the most important single measure of success of a commercial organization, the NCB has done much more than just make a profit. NCB has honored its role in Corporate Social Responsibility. The philosophy of the bank is important to the development of the banking system; the main objective is to change the structure of banking through its own influence, through its policies and practices, and not by means of any physical acquisitions of other banks.

The philosophy of the NCB stands on three main

pillars. Firstly, the Bank has to be competitive with the foreign banks in terms of interest rates, charges, and services and yet must maintain the highest standards of financial principles. Secondly, the Bank intends to make the credit policies and practices of the banking system more favorable to the people of Trinidad and Tobago without endangering the deposits of its customers. Thirdly, the Bank through its operations will continue to provide advisory and counseling services to its customers and the community at large so as to explode the mystery surrounding banking.

Prime Minister's undertaking

When the first Board of Directors were appointed, they were given an oral undertaking by Prime Minister, Dr. the Rt. Honorable Eric E. Williams that there would not be any political interference in the operations of NCB.

The Prime Minister honored his undertaking up to his death. There was just one occasion when one of his Ministers wrote to Board Members individually seeking to direct them on a matter relating to the operations of the Bank. A letter was sent to the Prime Minister signed by all the members of the Board enquiring whether a new policy was being implemented contrary to the undertaking the Prime Minister had given them on their initial appointment.

The result was that the errant Minister called the Board to his office, withdrew the letter and apologized to the Board. The Minister said in his defense to the Prime Minister and to the Board that he was under the mistaken impression that the subject matter had been agreed to between his Permanent Secretary and the Chief Executive of NCB. This was an apparent end to the matter.

As a result of board expansion and the resignation, retirement, or death of original directors, other directors appointed were Dr. Alma Jordan, Librarian; Dr. Claude Denbow, S.C. Attorney-at-law; Mr. Frank Rampersad, Economist and former Permanent Secretary, Ministry of Finance; Mr. Samuel Martin former Senior Economist and former Director of Project Planning, Ministry of Finance; Dr. Norbert Masson, Engineer and former Head of Department John Donaldson Technical Institute; Dr. Aleem Mohammed, President, S. M. Jaleel & Company; Executive directors were Mr. Ganace Ramdial, Mr. Andrew McEachrane, Mr. Michael Warner, Mr. Alfred Gopaulsingh, and Mr. Lennard Prescod.

These additional appointments of Board Members, from time to time, strengthened, deepened and broadened the skills and experience of the original Board Members.

New Board Policy Appointment

The appointment of two board members who had previous direct relationships with the Government at very senior level appointments in the public service was a new development. Some persons viewed this as an opening for political intrusion in NCB.

This public fear of possible political intrusion was reflected in one of the local Newspapers, The Challenge, and one of its columnist's at the time, Mr. Louis Lee Sing, commented in its issue of January 06 1982 at page 5. Mr. Lee Sing reflected the views of many persons that it was not in the best interests of the Bank to have Government Agents on it.

Post-appointment experience of
Government Agents

Fortunately, the fear of political interference did not occur. There were spasmodic attempts by individual politicians in a non-structured manner but these initiatives failed. There were four major reasons why NCB was a bulwark against political interference at an operational level:

[1] The experience, knowledge, and banking expertise of the other Board Members outweighed that of the agents.

[2] The Managers of the NCB remained faithful to follow the tenets and principles of commercial banking.

[3] The general staff of NCB were loyal to their bank.

[4] The threat that the minority shareholders of NCB, that numbered over 23,000 persons, would make their voices heard in opposition to political interference, during the Annual General Meeting that at law had to be held annually.

Appointment of NCB'S Executives to the Board

The creeping political intrusion had another consequence. The non-Executive members of the Board felt strongly against political interference and intimated that they would resign 'in block' if such intervention was intolerable. If this did occur the bank would be without a board and NCB.S operations would be adversely affected, during the period that a new Board was being appointed by Cabinet. For example, credit facilities beyond the limit of executive management, and only within the authority of the board, would not be able to be finalized.

The constitution of the Bank required four members of the Board to form a quorum. Accordingly, the Chairman proposed and the Annual General Meeting agreed to the expansion of the Board by four additional full-time executives of the bank. Thus, the Executive Chairman and the four other full-time executives would ensure that a quorum of four members of the Board would always be available.

In NCB'S Twelfth Annual Report at page 9 the change is explained as follows: "We have expanded the Board from 8 to 12, four of whom are full-time executives. This important innovation in terms of publicly controlled enterprises, has given the bank the necessary capability to respond quickly and appropriately to the needs of its customers and to enable the NCB to be innovative in banking in this community. As Chairman, I wish to commend the Board once more for the strategic part it continues to play in the successful development of the bank."

CHAPTER 3

COMMUNICATION MODEL DEVELOPED FOR NATIONAL COMMERCIAL BANK

The Communication Framework

The five major pillars of the bank's mission: were
  • confidentiality • convenience • competence
  • customer delight and • computerization.

These five Pillars all begin with the letter "C", and have as their foundation a sixth word beginning with the same letter—Communication. The Communication Framework is the fundamental platform on which the five Pillars of the Bank stand, and that integrates the five Pillars.

Communication is the glue that holds an organization together. The people in an organization are from different backgrounds, and have different values and goals for their lives. This provides a setting for disharmony that has to be remedied through proper use of effective communication. The mission of the bank can be the unifying business focus.

Where the mission is clear and powerful, the organization's members can be committed to its achievement. The business mission then becomes the rallying point to unite the organization against external factors. The enemy is outside the organization; the enemy is not between the individuals, sections and departments within its own borders.

Effective communications make the mission, core values, strategic direction, goals, policies and procedures become a living reality. This led to NCB developing a Communication Framework. NCB'S declared mission was "To be the best bank in the Country." This was further explained as being the best in: (a) customer service (b) return to shareholders (c) staff remuneration (d) products & services, and (e) corporate social responsibility." This was later refined to: "To be the leading relevant, financial institution in Trinidad and Tobago, effected through a properly trained and sensitive staff."

The Culture Trap

Trinidad and Tobago is made up of many races, religions, different political persuasions, and different cultures. This is so central to the Country that its Constitution requires that every creed and race find an equal place. The National Commercial Bank being a microcosm of the Country, great care had to be taken to avoid disturbing individual cultural sensibilities.

Thus, to develop the culture of the organization required skilful handling of the formulation of the bank's culture through using the Communication Model.

Elements of the Framework

Arising from the importance of communication, NCB developed a Communication Framework for all stakeholders with special reference to employees. The employees' framework consisted primarily of these elements, and some examples of them will be also given:

- Managing Director's Circular monthly to each member of staff
- Managers' Weekly from the Managing Director to all managers weekly
- Monthly Magazine, NATCOMVIEW, bringing the staff up-to-date

- 'Interface' publication integrating branch and interpersonal communications
- 'Business Information' publication to encourage the staff's creative expression in relation to banking matters, directly and indirectly

Managing Director's Circular to celebrate 16 years

On 30 June 1986 the following circular was sent to each staff member:

"Dear Staff Members

"Congratulations on being part of a successful banking organization. On 1986 July 01, we celebrate sixteen (16) years of building an effective, successful and profitable organization. We have been relevant to the community, helpful to our customers and developed the personal and career growth of the bank's staff.

"The members of staff of the bank were cumulatively responsible for our pride of success. It is our very staff that holds the future of the bank in their hands. It is only by the committed, dedicated and excellent service by the staff that we can maintain what our indigenous organization has demonstrated to the nation. It is therefore useful to re-visit some of the features that have helped to guide our National Bank successfully. These criteria can be conveniently summarized as:—

- the Bank's mission
- the Bank's basis
- the Bank's purpose
- the Bank's Creed and
- the Bank's ten (10) corporate principles.

"THE BANK'S MISSION

"NCB'S mission is to be the leading relevant financial institution in Trinidad and Tobago effected through a properly trained and sensitive staff. (See "Interface" Vol.2 of 1985 – front cover)

"THE BANK'S BASIS

"The Bank's basis is personnel effectively meeting the financial needs of customers. (See "Interface" Vol. 5 of 1985 – page 4)

"THE BANK'S PURPOSE

"The ESSENCE of NATIONAL COMMERCIAL BANK is three fold:—

"Firstly, it must satisfy the financial and business needs of our customers.

Secondly, the bank must provide opportunities in personal growth for its staff and be fair and just in its dealings with staff.

Thirdly, the services of the bank must be delivered to the customers with excellence and cost effectiveness by the staff. (See "Interface" Vol. 2 of 1986 page 2 and Vol. 3 of 1986 – cover)

"THE BANK'S CREED

"The NCB Creed is expressed as:—

- A. Every individual must be respected: this respect extends to each other on the job, the customers and the general public
- B. The customer must always be treated courteously and given the best possible service
- C. Excellence in the job and consistent superior job performance must be pursued. (See "Interface" Vol. 5 of 1986 – page 2)

"NCB'S CORPORATE PRINCIPLES

"The ten (10) NCB Corporate Principles are:—

(1) Prioritize your daily activities and do the most productive thing at every given moment

(2) Be vigilant and contribute personally.

(3) Show integrity, respect and fairness to others.

(4) Cultivate and maintain the highest corporate financial standards.

(5) Have pride, purpose, mission and knowledge about your job.

(6) Extend courteous and efficient service to customers at all times.

(7) Always give reliable information.

(8) Encourage, foster and follow an "open-door" policy to subordinates.

(9) Communicate with understanding and respect.

(10) Support and give positive reinforcement to others in the bank.

(See "Interface" Vol. 4 of 1985 page 2 and Vol. 12 of 1985 – inside page of back cover)

"We can do no better than to consider the notation on the cover of "Interface" Vol.2 of 1986 which reads as follows:—

"PRIDE, DEDICATION, CONTINUED COMMITMENT and TOMORROW'S ACCOMPLISHMENTS in the job will ensure the financial success of the National Commercial Bank and each employee's success as well."

"Finally, we have worked hard and well in the past sixteen years but the stringent economic times require us to work even harder in the future. Our commitment, resolve and persistency must be even stronger in the upcoming period. Our future is in our hands. Our shareholders are expecting us to honor that sacred trust which they have put in our hands.

"Happy Corporate Anniversary Celebrations.

Yours sincerely

Philip G. Rochford
Managing Director"

Board of Directors

The Board normally met twice in each month. The communication policy adopted by Executive Management towards the Board was three fold. First, there must be full disclosure to the Board despite any untoward reflection on the staff; also, the banking legislation, especially as it related to Directors, had to be observed. Second, submissions to the Board must be "pressure proof" which is a concept that preparation must be so extensive that every enquiry by Board members must be answerable without difficulty. Third, the facts and opinions being placed before the Board must be able to stand positive scrutiny by a One-Man Commission of Enquiry.

The Bank's Customers

Quite apart from the general public branding pursued by the bank, customers were communicated with when strategic changes were being made to their accounts; and the various bank's publications were also available to them. The usual procedure of placing brochures in the banking halls, and including relevant information, where appropriate, with their monthly statements were also followed.

Shareholders

Communication with shareholders was sensitive. There was the clear communication pathway stipulated in the Companies Ordinance under which the NCB was incorporated. This gave the Board of Directors, 'qua Board', the legal governance of the company. However, as happens so often, a majority shareholder tends to want to overstep the boundaries of the legislation and interfere in the governance of the company. This breach is sometimes followed in a privately held company, but when the NCB became a public company with over 23,000 shareholders this was unacceptable.

In fact, this was also not acceptable when NCB first opened its doors with 100% Government shareholding. There was a countervailing balance in that from the start there were more customer deposits in the bank than the value of the Government's shareholding. There was thus a fiduciary trust by the bank for the preservation of depositors' funds. Perhaps the then Prime Minister, Dr. The Rt. Hon Eric Eustace Williams understood this, and gave the first Board an oral undertaking of non- political interference that he honored up to his death in March 1981.

CHAPTER 4

SIGNIFICANT ACHIEVEMENTS IN PRODUCT AND OPERATIONAL DEVELOPMENT

Customers' delight

The basic intention was to provide opportunities for customers to have access to products and services not then available that had the potential to improve their financial position.

Customer delight and bank profitability are tied together. One of the philosophies of the bank was that the bank exists to provide products and services that customers want and can pay for; the manner in which these services are provided by the staff will determine the profits that the bank makes. This means that the priority must be to delight the customer. If the customer is happy with the service, not only does the customer return but the bank has an ambassador who will recommend NCB to friends family and acquaintances, thereby extending the bank's market share.

Creation of New Products and Services

NCB'S analysis of the commercial banking market place revealed the following opportunities:

(a) small depositors could be given better deposit rates

(b) loans for house building were neglected

(c) facilitation of small and medium business loans was needed

(d) there appeared to be gender neglect in the case of females

(e) need for introduction of modern bank technology

(f) better returns for customers with large daily balances in non-interest bearing accounts

Long-term financing

The remit of a commercial bank does not include long-term housing mortgages, merchant banking, and lease financing. Thus, the National Commercial Bank needed to incorporate a Trust company, a merchant bank, and a leasing company. From an operational point of view establishing a joint venture merchant bank and leasing company with international banks were strategic imperatives.

An important aspect of satisfying customers'

needs must be the availability of a significant range of financial services. In pursuit of this objective various strategies were followed culminating in the establishment of the following organizations:

- 1975 February: Established a joint venture leasing company Trinfinance Limited with Citibank; and in 1985 January acquired Citibank's 40% shareholding in that leasing company, thereby making it a wholly owned subsidiary of NCB. Mr. Tyrone Tang was a key resource in developing Trinfinance Limited, and thus he was appointed its Manager

- 1979 June: Acquired the operations of Citibank's branch operations at Piarco International Airport, Trinidad.

- 1981 January: Acquired the operations of Chase Manhattan Bank for incorporation in the business of the National Commercial Bank of Trinidad and Tobago Limited.

- 1981 September: Established a joint venture with Bank de Paris des Pays-Bas (Paribas) to form an Industrial Merchant Bank, and in 1983 acquired the 40% shareholding of Paribas in that Industrial Merchant Bank to make it a wholly owned subsidiary of NCB. Mr. Alfred

Gopaulsingh, as the new Managing Director of the Industrial Merchant Bank expanded its operations and steered this merchant bank from losses to profitability.

The structural human resource imperative

This narrative gives a glimpse of some aspects of NCB'S internal workings. Customers have certain expectations, some external to the bank, and others within the bank's responsibility. What may not be always clear is, for instance, that on the one hand political stability, general civic conduct, business laws, and the like are a government's responsibility. On the other hand, banking convenience, customer confidentiality, bank operational competency, relevant products and services, and competitive value are some of the bank's responsibilities. Of course, there were the expectations of shareholders to receive adequate dividends and an increase in their share value.

Thus, some of the imperatives to establish a strong local commercial banking system were to:

[1] confirm the high level of customer confidentiality
[2] demonstrate competency to deliver the bank's products & services

[3] provide a network of branches to suit the convenience of customers

[4] develop new relevant products and services not otherwise available

One of the main challenges facing the National Commercial Bank was the misconception by the general public that customers' confidential bank business would be disclosed to Government agencies such as Inland Revenue Department and Central Bank. This view was held because the original government ownership was 100%.

This was a period of stringent exchange control during which foreign currency needed to be conserved by the country. Some people believed that the Central Bank would have access to their foreign transactions. Others felt that the Inland Revenue Department would be privy to their real profits. These were such widespread concerns that the Government's Advisor from Switzerland, Dr. Agathon Aerni, insisted that the new Bank should have a Board of independent-minded persons, as well as no civil servants nor active political supporters. Dr. Agathon Aerni's recommendations were accepted, and this proved very critical to bolstering the perception of the bank's confidentiality and viability.

In terms of local resources, NCB had an impressive Board and one that met the criteria of competence, experience, independent mindedness, and the absence of political ties. Also, the first Chairman, Mr. Cyril Duprey, set the lead, being a man of renowned financial probity.

The Management Team

A critical task was to build a cadre of management personnel who could efficiently set, guide, and supervise day-to-day operations. Edith Penrose in her book "The Theory of the Growth of the Firm" contends that the limit to the growth of a firm is the limit of the skills, training, and experience of members of the management team. Moreover, the limit is circumscribed by the weakest link on the team.

This management team concept led to a deliberate focus on building a strong management team at NCB. There were thirty-five members of staff inherited from BOLAM, but none of them had post-secondary qualifications. The expatriate on BOLAM'S staff returned to Canada within two month's of NCB'S establishment. Within thirty days, NCB'S Chief Executive recruited Attorney-at-law Mr. Ganace Ramdial and Chartered Secretary

Mr. Melville P. Lewis. They both had beneficial financial experience. (Years later Mr. Ramdial went on to become Chairman and Chief Executive of the Trinidad Co-operative Bank and thereafter President of the Senate of Parliament, and at times, by virtue of operation of law, Acting President of the Republic of Trinidad and Tobago. Mr. Melville P. Lewis was subsequently appointed Chief Executive of the Trinidad and Tobago Building and Loan Association.)

The Human Resource Element

For a bank to exist there must be persons who need its services, and staff to serve the customers. The critical element of staff was demonstrated at page 5 of the 6th Annual Report of NCB that stated 'inter alia'

"The human resource element is critical to the bank's survival and growth. In order to meet the challenge of the bank's physical and customer expansion it was necessary to develop staff quantitatively as well as in its quality.

"During the year the Bank and General Workers' Union (BGWU) received recognition as the Union representing the junior staff."

This was another strategic option followed by

NCB. The international banks in Trinidad and Tobago actively discouraged the formation of Trade Union representation for their banks' staff. NCB on the other hand did not discourage trade union representation for its staff. NCB'S concept was that the staff should have a countervailing balance of power to combat any improper actions by the bank's management or its supervisory staff. Additionally, trade union representation for a significant number of staff would ensure fairness in setting terms and conditions of employment that would eventually have the potential to redound to the benefit of sustained and increased productivity of the staff.

However, a management team is only relevant if there are persons to be managed. There were overall strategies established for the pursuit of policies for customer confidentiality, bank competence, customer delight and profitability. However, there had to be tactical interventions to manifest the respective outcomes. For example, in the case of customer confidentiality, apart from the independence and political neutrality of the Board of Directors, a system was developed to remind staff of their responsibility for customer secrecy, and a program of internal training was developed to focus on confidentiality.

Managerial staff was exposed to systematic meetings that incorporated the elements of customer confidentiality. For instance, merely mentioning to your next-door neighbor that his or her spouse was in the bank today was inappropriate. There was a case where that occurred but the neighbor did not know that her spouse had an account at that branch of the bank. This caused difficulties in the spouses' relationship.

A suite of internal training programs on the nature and determinants of customer confidentiality were developed and administered to all members of staff. Additionally, all staff members were required to sign to an oath of confidentiality every six months, with a reminder that any breach of customer confidentiality was a just cause for instant dismissal of the offending staff member.

The world is changing fast and knowledge is increasing. NCB had to establish a culture of life-long learning for its staff to keep abreast of worldwide developments in banking. Thus, NCB'S 8th Annual Report at page 5 states:

"The Bank continues to be conscious of the vital importance of maintaining adequate numbers of properly trained staff to handle its ever increasing business. We recruited key staff with a mixture of academic and professional training, and actual banking experience. The Bank has continued to train its existing staff both locally and overseas. Four staff members were sent in our eight financial year to the U.K. and the U.S.A. for training in international banking; and over 100 members of staff were trained locally in fields such as supervisory methods, communications, credit analysis, customer relations, accounting, corporate planning, and computer audit.

"Our 1977/1978 financial year which was specially designated "the year of training" for the Bank had, as a key element, the award of three scholarships by the Bank to junior members of its staff to pursue a degree course in Management Studies at the University of the West Indies, St. Augustine, which would be over a period of three years. This is the start of a Scholarship Program for the staff of the Bank, and the intention is to provide in the future, a flow of management staff from within the Bank to meet the expansion needs of the Bank. In this way, the career opportunities for persons leaving secondary school and joining the Bank would be assured, and staff can, at the point of entry from secondary school, aspire to the leadership of the Bank as long as they have shown their dedication, effectiveness, and competence.

"Once more, our entire staff must be congratulated for the way in which they have responded to the challenges of the job and of the changing dynamic nature of the environment."

NCB Learning Center

A pivotal strategy to ensure the continuing upgrading of employees' skills to match the growing needs of customers was the establishment of a full-scale internal Learning Center. This led to the building in Central Trinidad of the then most modern corporate training facility in the English Speaking Caribbean. Mr Nazeer Sultan, Corporate Manager, successfully implemented this construction project, as well as the human resource element of structured employees' training programs.

The structure included a mock bank, technology for simultaneous broadcasting in all the training rooms and a meditation or mindfulness room. This space for what is being referred to as mindfulness in the 21st Century was not a corporate buzzword in the 1970s and 1980s.

This space was available to every employee of NCB regardless of religion, creed, race, or color, and was particularly intended for use by employees of NCB who came from all parts of Trinidad and Tobago for training at the NCB Learning Center. There were three major rules for employees using the Meditation Room: (a) while in the space there should be no speaking; (b) there should be no noise disruption; and (c) no eating. In this way, employees could exercise their prayer, meditation, quiet time, silent chanting or any other esoteric practice of their choice. This provided for the possibility of mindfulness, and that the psychic space of another employee be not invaded while in this space provided for mindfulness.

This mindfulness space provided the oasis for employees to center their spirituality and physicality amidst the demands of customers' requirements, and the general stress of life.

A number of other appointments were made. Additionally, the bank instituted in-house operational banking training programs and initiated study leave and scholarship programs to encourage staff to make careers in banking.

Impact of NCB'S Training Philosophy

By the time of retirement of the first Chief Executive, twenty-three years after the bank started, there were more than eighty people with tertiary education in such fields as banking, accounting, information technology, law, administration, financing, and human resources—a figure that far outdistanced the staff make-up in any of the other banks in Trinidad and Tobago!.

Moreover, a number of employees trained at the National Commercial Bank eventually migrated to senior positions elsewhere in the corporate world, and governance of Trinidad and Tobago. For example: Mr. Andrew McEachrane went on to become Chairman of the Trinidad and Tobago Stock Exchange; Mr. Michael Alexander to Chief Executive, Unit Trust of Trinidad and Tobago; Mr. Keith Toby to Vice President, Iron and Steel Company of Trinidad and Tobago; Mr. John Ottley, to be a Member of the Integrity Commission of Trinidad and Tobago; Mr. Leroy Calliste to Financial Controller, RBTT; Mr. Larry Howai to Chief Executive, First Citizens Bank, and later Minister of Finance in a Government of The United National Congress; Mr. Arnold Piggott to Minister of Works, Minister of Foreign Affairs, and Minister of Agriculture, Lands and Marine Resources in a Peoples National Movement Government; Mr. Martin De Gannes to Human Resources Manager of Bank of Nova Scotia and President, of the Employers' Consultative Association; Mrs. Judith Morrain-Webb to Lecturer at the University of the West Indies; Mr. Lennard Prescod to Vice President, Finance and Procurement, University of Trinidad and Tobago; Mr. Nazeer Sultan to Executive Team Leader, CMMB Securities Limited; Mr. Gregory Thompson to Deputy Managing Director, Republic Bank; Ms. Hesper Peters to Regional Business Development Officer, CMMB Securities Limited; Mr. Anton Doldron to Manager, Bank of Montserrat Limited; Mr. Terrence O'Neil Lewis to Judge of the Tax Appeal Board; Mr. Latchmi Patasar to Chairman, Agricultural Development Bank; Mr. Michael Toney to Chairman, National Insurance Board; Mr. Philip Marshall to Chairman, Caribbean Airlines Limited; Mr. Vishnu Bholaisingh to Manager, JMMB Bank; Mrs. Donna Latiff to Head, Card Services, Bank of Nova Scotia; and Mr. Charles Mitchell to Chief Executive, North West Regional Health Authority. Of course, this is not a fully exhaustive list as there was no formal tracking system established.

Governance of Trinidad and Tobago

The establishment of National Commercial Bank was just one strand in developing the economy of

Trinidad and Tobago. At a fundamental level, the employees of NCB generally gave their attention, skill, training and experience in pursuing their employment responsibilities and accountabilities.

This led to a significant number of employees moving towards becoming the best expression of themselves. The outgrowth of their high performances fitted many of them, as shown above, to be appointed to governance positions in Trinidad and Tobago—a sterling contribution to Society by Managers of NCB. NCB prepared its employees for life beyond just a career in the Bank.

Better deposit rates for small depositors

How could the Bank influence skeptics and detractors to risk doing business with the Bank? One approach was to offer them an income advantage that they did not have at their existing bank without requiring them to change their main existing banking arrangements. To accomplish this, the bank marketed a unique product aimed at giving value to customers without them having to take great risk. The Bank institutionalized the Trinidad and Tobago homemade facility called *"sou sou"*.

The Chaconia account, as NCB'S product was christened, required a customer to agree to save a minimum of at least fifty dollars per month for twelve consecutive months. This entitled the customer to an effective interest rate of 7 percent per annum paid on monthly balances. No other bank at that time paid interest of 7 percent on such small amounts.

The hook of the plan was that it was similar to the local traditional *"sou sou"*, but customers got more money than they paid into the *"sou sou."* They did not pay "box" to the organizer, as was done in some cases, which meant that no money was deducted from their deposits. The disadvantage was that all participants only received their "hands" at the end of the *"sou sou,"* as they got the "last hand." In fact, customers got what they deposited with the bank, plus a rate of interest not available at any other competing bank.

This gave people an opportunity to put their toes into the NCB water. Not much of the customer's wealth was at risk, and he or she would be getting a rate of interest not available at another bank. In the process, the customer would gain an actual favorable experience in dealing with the new bank and would in time conduct more of his or her business at NCB.

The strategy worked well. The Chaconia account was so successful that later it was leveraged to grant, after a twelve-month maturity, loans of twice its accumulated value, repayable over a period of two years. The security was the deposits in the plan. Customers who had demonstrated an ability to make the monthly payments to the Chaconia account would most likely be able to continue with the same loan repayment, and the bank would not be at risk after a year since the original Chaconia account was held as security. This was a win-win situation for NCB and its customers.

Life Insured Savings Accounts

The Bank provided group life insurance coverage for its savings' customers; the customer did not have to pay the insurance premium, and the customer did not have to undergo a medical examination. When introduced by NCB, this facility was not available at any other bank in Trinidad and Tobago.

To qualify for this life insurance coverage, the customer had to maintain a minimum quarterly balance of $600 for two consecutive quarters. On the death of the customer, in addition to the amount in the account, NCB paid a similar amount to the Estate of the deceased by virtue of the group life insurance coverage.

This program helped the growth of total deposits

at NCB from $4.5 million in the first year in1970 to over $1.5 billion in its final year in 1993.

Better terms for loans for house building

One of NCB'S marketing strategies was to find a unique market niche with a need and strong demand, then pursue it relentlessly. One such target area has already been mentioned. For customers who were sitting on the fence, fearful to take a risk with the new bank, the Chaconia account provided a product no other bank operating in Trinidad and Tobago marketed. The other main product that was neglected by the international banks related to financing of houses.

Home ownership

In 1970 the average person could not easily own a house for two reasons: first, trust companies of commercial banks lent mainly trustee funds for long term mortgages, and the enabling legislation permitted a maximum mortgage of two-thirds of the value of the property; and second, the foreign banks were not keen on investing in property due to the possibility that they might have to leave the country for one reason or another. Real estate as security was neither movable out of the country nor easily disposed for true value when, through special circumstances, required to be sold urgently.

Three initiatives were devised at NCB in the house mortgage arena. First, long-term fixed deposits, as opposed to Trustee funds were used by the bank's trust company to take a seventy-five percent first mortgage on the property. Second, the income of women was taken into account in determining the loan-service capability of husband and wife.

At that time the commercial banks did not ordinarily include a wife's income even though she might have been a professional in her own right! NCB introduced the policy that a female's income would qualify, if she were a professional or, alternatively, had been in permanent employment for the previous five years.

The third initiative was that, if an applicant's income allowed it, a further fifteen percent was given by the commercial bank itself—as opposed to the trust company—on a second mortgage on the property over five years. In 1970, all interest paid on mortgages was tax-deductible. This provided a good opportunity for newly graduated professionals who had large salaries were making large income tax payments but did not have accumulated savings to meet the twenty-five percent down payment requirement. The borrower thus financed a significant part of the mortgage repayment through an income tax reduction.

Eventually, the catchment of recent graduates was exhausted; others could not afford the five-year second mortgage. It was time to shift to another track. The bank's policy to require a prospective homeowner to have a deposit of only ten percent was so compelling that NCB approached an insurance company with the proposal to insure the top fifteen percent of the ninety percent mortgage, with the insurance company's risk terminating when the loan was paid down to seventy-five percent. Customers were thus able to get ninety percent mortgage financing that was affordable, and not available at any other financial institution. The National Insurance Board supported this policy, and subsequently ninety percent mortgage financing became standard in the market place.

NCB Trust Company

The NCB Trust Company was a wholly owned subsidiary of the National Commercial Bank and carried out the Trustee Services of the Bank. In carrying out the granting of mortgages for housing, the NCB Trust Company, in its 23 years of operations, granted one house mortgage every two days. This was a phenomenal achievement that positively changed the face of home ownership in Trinidad and Tobago.

Land loans

There was also a sub-niche in the housing market. Some people could not acquire a house immediately, but they could purchase land to build on later. A five-year loan of ninety percent of the value of the land would be approved by NCB to purchase the land, using the land as security. The customer was then encouraged to go ahead with the design process for the house. Usually, in two to three years his or her income would increase; the value of the land would increase; and a mortgage letter of commitment could be obtained. The bank would already have had a mortgage on the property, so bridging finance could be accessed with stringent oversight by the bank's panel of Quantity Surveyors.

Loans for tertiary education

Government's policy moved towards improving social mobility through free or assisted education.

However, the Dollar for Dollar education program where the government matched the student's investment, dollar for dollar, came into existence in 2001. Its successor, Government Assistance for Tertiary Education (GATE), where the Government provided full tuition to the student was introduced in 2004.

Prior to these two programs, the Government provided special funds issued to it by the Inter-American Development Bank to be loaned, on favorable terms, to students for their further education. These student loans were repayable by the students after their graduation. The National Commercial Bank was designated as the Financial Agent to administer the Students' Revolving Loan Fund. By 1986 NCB had made more than 1,269 student loans under this program. See "Interface" NCB publication Volume 5 1986.

After its establishment in September 1993, First Citizens Bank Limited was designated to act as the Financial Agent of this Fund by Trinidad and Tobago Gazette (Extraordinary) No.261 dated October 26 1993.

Introduction of modern bank technology

In 1970 the commercial banks in Trinidad and Tobago had not yet computerized their operations.

They were using mainly mechanical machines for their operations. There was a need to introduce computerization to NCB but since there was no example by the other banks, some members of NCB'S management team were reluctant to go that route of new technology. The problem was solved by sending, in rotation, members of the management team for training overseas at the bank's various Correspondent Banks in the United States and the United Kingdom, where the team saw computerization of operations of commercial banks in action. There was then full 'buy in' for computerization that led to NCB being the leader in Information Technology within the commercial banking sector of Trinidad and Tobago.

The Sixth Annual Report of NCB at page 3 it is stated:

"The growth of the bank's business and its increasing complexity has led to the installation of an IBM System 3 Model 8 Computer. The data processing of the bank's operations needed to be speeded up. The management required to get data fast, timely and relevant to remain competitive and this is being achieved through electronic data processing. The manual system is still in operation but the computer system is being run parallel in some of our operations until the computer system has been fully tested.

"It is the intention to open all new branches with the computer system in operation and to convert existing branches in a phased manner. The management has already seen tremendous benefits from the new computer technology. The staff would be relieved from the tedious but necessary calculations of interest on deposits and on loans, and of the necessity of spending long hours to construct data needed by the management to solve day-to-day problems arising outside the normal routines of the bank. The management also now has the flexibility of using modern concepts of model building in planning the operations of the bank, in policy formulation and in the adaptation of its marketing strategies. Our computer innovation is also offering new career opportunities for the staff of the bank."

It is noteworthy that Mr. Lennox G. Phillip, Corporate Manager, Data Processing was with the bank from the inception of the computerization program, and he was the ballast and consistent mainstay that facilitated NCB'S information technology supremacy in the banking industry of Trinidad and Tobago.

Some of the Other Supportive Staff

Some key operational areas

Four of the key operational areas were accounting, informational technology, branches, credit, and human resources. It was very important that the leadership performed effectively in these areas.

Mr. Lennard P. Prescod, Senior General Manager, was not only highly effective in his craft, but was considered the local Czar of the knowledge and interpretation of International Accounting Standards.

Mr. Keith Toby was the officer who was the guardian of the accounting function in the early life of NCB. Later on, Mr. Michael Toney, Head of the internal audit function strengthened and developed its framework, including establishing the operational manual for the Bank's internal audit function.

Mr. Leroy Calliste was the critical support in the accounting function as the Bank's growth exploded.

Mr. Lennox Phillip, Manager Data Processing, anchored and stabilized the Bank's Information Technology.

Mrs. Annette De Silva was one of the original employees of the bank, and became the first Female NCB Branch Manager, and she later was appointed one of the Area Managers in charge of a selected cluster of branches.

Mrs. Laura Cozier, Area Manager South/East/Tobago was trained and experienced in critical areas of the bank's operations, and that facilitated her functions in charge of dedicated branches.

Mr. Raymond Crichton, Manager Credit Administration, quietly and effectively supported the building and strengthening of the credit function in NCB.

Mr. Martin de Gannes, Corporate Manager Human Resources, steadied the human resources outgrowth, and ensured an effective framework for delivery of the bank's services. He further developed and strengthened the structure of the Human Resources Policies, and ensured their successful implementation.

Mr. Nazeer Sultan established and implemented the framework for the manpower planning function of NCB.

Mr. Neville Sandy kept a steady hand throughout his employment, in carrying out the important function of internal audit of NCB.

Mr. Clive Vieira was a steadying influence in the bank. He was the most senior officer of the 34 local employees recruited from the predecessor

Bank of London and Montreal. Mr. Vieira became a branch manager, corporate secretary to the Board, and Inspector of NCB'S Branches.

Mr. Arnold Piggott obtained significant experience and made a special contribution by being Manager of the NCB largest branch at Independence Square, Manager of the NCB Trust Company, Manager, Park Street Branch, and Executive Assistant to the Managing Director.

Mr. Joseph Pierre, Credit Specialist, was one of the commercial banking stalwarts from Chase Manhattan Bank's operations in Trinidad and Tobago that NCB acquired in January 1981.

Mr. Patrick Kelly, Manager, was a key support in the general administration of NCB.

As the bank grew, it became necessary to formalize our strategic plan. One of our highly trained key executives in planning, Ms. Hesper Peters, was designated Corporate Planner, and she pioneered NCB'S new hardware telephone technology that automated the system. Thus the executive team developed a system to ensure "quality telephone etiquette" throughout the branches.

Mrs. Judith Morrain-Webb was an effective branch manager and she was given the responsibility for monitoring the quality of delivery of the bank's customer service. This included being a mystery telephone caller to the various branches of the bank to test the staff's telephone response. Elements of the system extended to the maximum number of times the phone should ring before being answered, the precise words to be used on answering, and the tone of voice to be used. Training was also given on the technique to be used in transferring a call from one person or department to another, so that the customer does not have to repeat the same issue to several different persons. In her role as Customer Quality Manager she made anonymous calls to test the efficacy of the system.

Customers were surprised at the international-standard response they got when they called the bank. Some reported wondering whether they were in another country. The general public commended the bank for such a first in the banking industry.

An internal NCB target was to establish the bank as a good corporate citizen while not following the beaten path of the foreign banks. One plank in such a construct was to support groups that were not traditionally helped by the other banks, especially those that were income-challenged, with no "fairy godparent," or that were ignored for being rural.

NCB was proactive in this endeavor, and the targeted groups welcomed the new possibilities that NCB offered.

Ms. Indra Dorman, one of the 34 initial employees of NCB provided quiet efficient loyal service to NCB and was appointed one of our Managers.

As the bank became established and accepted, the Government divested 49% of its shares to the public and this resulted in some 23,000 members of the public becoming shareholders. The Government kept 51% majority ownership to avoid a takeover by private interests with financial resources who may not be primarily concerned with developing National Commercial Banking.

Specialist certification in commercial banking

NCB'S operations were essentially that of banking. Thus, while it was necessary to have employees trained in diverse professional and academic fields, a core of specialists in the operational intricacies of banking were also available.

There were eighty employees with tertiary level certification, but ten of these employees were certified by the Chartered Institute of Bankers: Mr. Brian D'Abreau, ACIB., Mr. Mario Young, ACIB., Mr. Egberrt Lewis, ACIB., Mr. Ivan Farinha, ACIB.,

Mrs. Chandradai Maharaj, ACIB., Mrs. Trixie Guy, ACIB., Mr. Gerald Phillip, ACIB., Mr. Lennard Prescod, FCIB., Mr. Ganace Ramdial, FCIB.,and Mr.Philip Rochford, FCIB.

NCB IS AMBUSHED

On 9th April 1989 the Central Bank closed the Workers' Bank and took control of it under the relevant banking legislation.

Unfortunately, a senior bank official from another commercial bank spread a rumor that the Central Bank was imminently also going to close the National Commercial Bank. This rumor took currency and significant deposits started to be withdrawn from NCB. There were two factors that permitted NCB to withstand the withdrawals and repay customers' deposits on demand.

Firstly, the international commercial banks' liquidity standards were being observed by NCB, so that cash was available to honor the withdrawals. Secondly, in January 1988, NCB had introduced a strategy of "Relationship Banking" and this included management staff, as a matter of weekly routine, visiting customers' places of business to serve them rather than the customers having to visit the bank. Thus, when some customers wanted to withdraw their deposits they contacted their relationship officer for guidance.

There was one NCB Manager who frantically called the Managing Director with tears in her eyes. She related that she had assured a customer that his $200,000 fixed deposit was safe, and he told her that if he lost it he would visit her with a cutlass in his hand. The Managing Director assured his Manager that all was well. There were many customer enquiries of the bank checking whether their deposits were safe but without the threats of violence, if their deposits were lost.

The Managing Director of NCB investigated the source of the rumor, and being satisfied of the source, reported the matter in writing to the Overseas Head Office of the offending senior banker. The Head Office replied apologizing and indicating that they did not condone such behavior and mandated their senior bank official to visit the Managing Director in person and apologize.

The offending senior bank officer did indeed in person visit the Managing Director. The offending senior bank officer explained that a senior officer of the Central Bank whom he trusted gave the information to him. Thus, he truly believed that his source was reliable. That was the end of the matter.

A possible fundamental mistake

No human being is perfect. There is in addition the adage that, "the asset is also the liability." Thus, in an accounting balance sheet, the assets must equal the liabilities.

A possible weakness in NCB'S progress was that the Chairman and Managing Director, Mr. Philip G. Rochford, did not explain sufficiently, to at least his Executive Management Team, ALL the underlying reasons for the competitive policies and strategies that the bank pursued.

It is true that while some justification was given to the management team for adoption of the bank's competitive policies and practices, there was implicit danger in disclosing too much information. Trinidad and Tobago is a relatively small society with friends and family being shared between all the competing banks, so great care had to be taken with the flow of information.

NCB'S success was dependent on outmaneuvering the competition. It was important that the competitive banks did not unwittingly get advanced information on the proposed strategies of NCB. Moreover, when the strategies were publicly unveiled, the competition should not be able to understand every aspect for its basis.

For example, the advertising program of NCB was vastly different than that of the other competitive banks. When customers of the other banks started to engage their banks about the novelty of NCB'S advertising, the competition called in their advertising agencies for conversations. They came to the conclusion that NCB was not following traditional bank advertising and that NCB'S approach should not be followed.

What was not understood was that the visuals in the advertisements represented items with which customers and potential customers could identify and be in empathy with—a loaf of bread; an ear of corn; a penknife; and images that reflected local empathy. Not even the Executive Management Team, as a Team, were privy to such secrets, and that kept the surprise and mystery of NCB'S initiatives.

There is no doubt that the Chairman and Managing Director had not fully communicated all the underlying reasons and strategic thinking for the adoption of particular strategies; had this been done there would likely have been more active support and passionate observance by the Executive Management Team.

There were two choices available to the Chairman and Managing Director:

[A] Partial disclosure to the Executive Management Team of all the deep underlying reasons for competitive policy formation, and thus not providing for the Team's fullest understanding and support of the policies.

[B] Full disclosure to the Executive Management Team of the underpinnings of competitive policy formation, and run the risk, through the contiguity of the Society, that the international competitive banks could sabotage or nullify NCB'S policies before they could become effective.

The best that can be said is that the Chairman and Managing Director of NCB held the view that the choice of [A] above was the lesser of the two evils.

Profits

The generation of profits is necessary for the continued survival of a business. It is really a residual figure and is determined by the efficacy of the policies, practices, and procedures of the organization.

In the case of the National Commercial Bank, regard must be paid to particular objectives in its formation, as it is related to profits. NCB was a commercial entity competing in a matured banking industry dominated by international commercial banks.

However, NCB was expected to fill certain gaps that the international banks were not serving. For instance, better deposit rates for small depositors, more business loans to new and inexperienced business entrepreneurs, better support to sports and cultural activities, developing in a massive manner technical and managerial executive staff, and implementing qualitative changes in the banking and financial system. All these elements are costly. Thus, while initially the generation of profits was necessary, such profits could not be super-profits, but optimal profits that were not obscene.

There needed to be profits adequate to meet the legitimate expectations of stakeholders. The shareholders had to get an adequate return on their shares. The workers should be properly compensated. Customers must not be charged excessive interest, rates and charges. The Government must get its fair share of taxes. The Community outreach must be adequate.

Reinvestment must be made in the bank to maintain and grow its market share. All these factors and more have to be taken into account when assessment of profitability is taken into account.

The profits profile of NCB follows:

National Commercial Bank – Consolidated Profit before taxation for year ended June 30 TT$ 000

1971	1972	1973	1974	1975	1976	1977	1978	1979	1980	1981
209	356	858	819	1033	2112	3216	5423	6702	4858	11805

1982	1983	1984	1985	1986	1987	1988	1989	1990	1991	1992
11557	13865	13733	8317	12557	3450	3975	5552	6237	6938	7980

Beyond just profits

There is no denying the necessity for profits: it provides the opportunity to reward investors, and facilitates the continuance and growth of the organization. This being said, it must be recognized that there is also an obligation to impact the wider society to which the organization owes its continued existence—hence the concept of Corporate Social Responsibility.

This is a key responsibility of the leader of the organization. It is his/her remit to balance the interests of all stakeholders, including the community. The mandate of the company and the environment of society define the boundaries for corporate social initiatives.

The Challenge of Leadership

Leaders are always challenged because the followers and naysayers do not all have the "Admiral's view of the fleet." The "Leadership Challenge" has existed from time immemorial. Note that in ancient times Moses was leading the children of Israel out of Egypt to Canaan. A capsule of the journey is indicated in Deuteronomy Ch. 32. This was a journey normally of eleven days. However, the journey took forty years, and according to the dominant view of commentators, this delay was due primarily to the negative attitude displayed by the followers towards Moses' leadership.

Leadership is quite complex, as outlined in the author's book "Enlightened Corporate Leadership" (2013). At pages 46 to 50 of this Leadership Book, author Philip G. Rochford observes:

"Leadership defined

"There are many different definitions of leadership and some of the dominant ones follow:

- Leadership is the element that directly and intentionally has the responsibility for the growth and direction of an entity.
- Leadership is a function of (1) competencies and personal qualities (2) desired results and (3) effective emotional intelligence. Each of these three areas is critical, but no area by itself is sufficient to constitute enlightened leadership.
- Leadership is a serious meddling in the lives of others, to provide the benefits the followers need, through the service undertaken by the leader.
- Leadership consists of a set of skills that are inherited, but the skills can also be acquired through life-long learning coupled with a competitive drive.

"Who is a Leader

"A Leader is someone you follow because you are attracted to his/her vision, values and integrity. You follow the leader out of your choice rather than through narrow necessity for favor in your life. Leadership is assessed by the premises, beliefs and human understanding rather than through techniques, tools, and systems. A sign of good leadership is whether the followers are reaching their potential

"Leadership can be gauged by the tone of the followers. Are the followers reaching their potential, achieving the desired results, managing conflict, and adapting to change?

"A Leader has to come from the crowd that he/she leads. By the same token, the leader has to be ahead of the crowd to be their leader, and must also not be so far ahead that the crowd ceases to follow. Critical elements of a leader must be a clear sense of self, knowing the reality of the situation, an understanding of the needs and values of the followers and serving them, a powerful communicator, and an image of integrity.

"Guidelines leaders use to maintain effective leadership:

- their approach to facilitate the generation of creative work
- they provide the space for creative people to be fruitful
- they take care to balance the rigidity of the rules of the organization, with thinking outside the box

"Three common mistakes that leaders make are:

[1] They stop learning, believing that they know it all.
[2] They fail to adapt to new technology.
[3] They become complacent

"Leader's role

"The ultimate role of a leader is to satisfy his/ her followers. To accomplish this, the leader has to know what the followers need and want. This has to be expressed as measurable results. This is not always easily determined and there are various processes that can be used to obtain feedback from the followers. Unless there is a fit between what the followers perceive as their need and what the leader considers to be the vision and goals of the followers, there will be a breakdown in the leader/follower relationship.

"The desired results may be expressed in generic terms but there must be a conversion to measurable outcomes. For example, one desired result may be water availability for the population. Looked at more specifically, you may say potable water for 75% of the population for 360 days in a calendar year, potable water for15% of the population 5 days per week, and for the remaining 10% of the population potable water 3 days per week.

"In this way, both the leader and the followers will be able to determine objectively the effectiveness of the leader with respect to this particular desired result of water availability for the population."

Leadership evidence

What evidence is there of NCB'S leadership? One of the measures is to track how NCB'S employees impacted on moving Trinidad and Tobago forward. The employees were so groomed and nurtured that many of them subsequently held pivotal positions of governance in Trinidad and Tobago.

Some examples of high office subsequently held by previous employees of NCB were acting President of Trinidad and Tobago; President of the Senate of Trinidad and Tobago; Deputy Managing Director of the largest commercial Bank(Republic Bank) in Trinidad and Tobago; Chief Executive of the Unit Trust of Trinidad and Tobago; Judge of the Tax Appeal Board; Member of the Integrity Commission; Minister of Foreign Affairs; Chairman of Caribbean Airlines Limited; Chairman of the Stock Exchange; Chairman of the National Insurance Board; Minister of Finance; Director of Petrotrin; Vice President

University of Trinidad and Tobago; President of the Employers' Consultative Association; Vice-President, Iron and Steel Company; Chairman Agricultural Bank. Financial Controller Royal Bank of Trinidad and Tobago; Chief Executive, North West Regional Health Authority; and this is not an exhaustive list.

It is undisputable that NCB, among the business organizations, provided the development of the most human resources for building the capacity for the future good governance of the Country. Thus, the success of NCB has to be measured beyond the narrow confines of organizational profits.

Corporate Social Responsibility in Trinidad & Tobago

It is interesting that in the Trinidad Express Newspapers of August 20 2013, there is an article headlined: "Towards a Corporate Social Responsibility Policy for Trinidad & Tobago." The article states in part as follows:

"A good company delivers excellent products and services, and a great company does all that and strives to make the world a better place." –William Ford Jr, chairman, Ford Motor Co.

"In recent years, there has been a noted shift in the way companies operate. Companies are taking stock of their social, as well as economic impact, and are starting to look beyond the bottom-line. Many companies today are recognizing the benefits of engaging in Corporate Social Responsibility (CSR) practices.

"CSR is about how business takes account of its economic, social, and environmental impacts, and encompasses the voluntary actions that a company can take, over and above compliance with minimum legal requirements, to address both its competitive interests and the interests of the wider society.

ISO 26000 defines social responsibility as "the responsibility of an organization for the impacts of its decisions and activities on society and the environment, that through transparent and ethical behavior:

- contributes to sustainable development, including health and the welfare of society;
- takes into account the expectations of stakeholders;
- is in compliance with applicable law and consistent with international norms of behavior; and
- is integrated throughout the organization and practiced in its relationships."

"How a company responds to its social responsibility affects the economy, society and the environment. A holistic approach according to the ISO standard would encompass corporate governance policies on community involvement and development, human rights, consumer issues, labor practices, fair operating practices and the environment.

"Most of the CSR activities in developing countries are mainly performed by western multinational corporations. The same can be said of Trinidad and Tobago. However, to achieve sustainable development in Trinidad and Tobago, which fosters a better quality of life for everyone, an integrated approach to social progress, economic growth, employment and environmental protection must be attained.

"CSR addresses all of these aspects and it is therefore crucial for organizations to adopt business activities that deliver economic, social and environmental benefits. Besides the overall national benefit CSR offers, companies can . . . . . ."

Towards a National Policy on Corporate Social Responsibility

At the time of writing this book, no Government in the history of Trinidad and Tobago formulated and proclaimed a Legislative Framework National Policy on "Corporate Social Responsibility (CSR)." It is hoped that this will be done by 2030, as the Country needs it.

CHAPTER 5

COMMUNITY OUTREACH FOR DEVELOPING SOCIETY

Selective large viable loans

Financing large loans intended for the benefit of the Country at large was another operational strategy. As previously noted, the foreign banks were not keen on financing home mortgages or land loans for building houses. Thus, for similar reasons, they were not interested in financing large tracks of land for Industrial and Commercial Estate Development.

Consequently, the long-standing dream of Southern Magnates to develop the Point Lisas Industrial Estate (PLIPDECO) was not being realized. In the 1950's under the drive of Mr. Robert Montano some momentum occurred. Eventually, on September 16 1966, Point Lisas Industrial Port Development Corporation (PLIPDECO) was incorporated.

In the early1970's the South Chamber of Industry and Commerce accepted the Government's offer to become a major shareholder, and subsequently PLIPDECO became a State Enterprise. Enter NCB!

NCB considered that the PLIPDECO publicly declared project of a deep-water harbor, and the use of PLIPDECO'S extensive flat land, in Central Trinidad, for diversification and reconstruction of the economy as worthwhile. Fortunately, the Government through its Advisor for the PLIPDECO Project, accepted an NCB proposal for the capital structuring of PLIPDECO. This Cabinet agreement permitted construction work to begin and gave the assurance to many potential tenants of the Estate that they could plan to locate at PLIPDECO. Many of these potential customers had already indicated publicly that they may have had to look elsewhere to locate, as many years had passed with no significant visible action being undertaken at the PLIPDECO Estate.

This was a significant intervention by NCB to facilitate the new birth of PLIPDECO through providing a creative financing capital structure that enabled construction of the Estate to move forward in earnest. Mr. Ganace Ramdial, Deputy Managing Director of NCB, as a Director of PLIPDECO, looked primarily after safeguarding the interests of National Commercial Bank's financing of PLIPDECO.

Branch Network

There was much debate by detractors that the bank's method and rate of branch expansion were flawed. Research conducted in the United States of America had established that convenience of banking location was a decisive factor in a customer's selection of a bank. Accordingly, National Commercial Bank's original strategy was to establish five branches in five years and ten branches in ten years. Mr. Ganace Ramdial, originally second in command at NCB, had as one of his responsibilities the establishment and control of the Branch network of NCB. Moreover, Mr. Ramdial being then the only Attorney-at-law on the Bank's staff, was the internal pivotal staff member with the responsibility for legal matters relating to NCB'S overall operations.

Subsequently, Mr. Andrew Mc Eachrane, Deputy Managing Director and Chief Operating Officer succeeded Mr. Ramdial in the Bank's branch network expansion function.

Some commentators felt strongly that such branch expansion was too speedy. They simply did not grasp that branches had to be developed quickly, if NCB were to increase its one percent share of the market. Further, to lay claim as a "National Bank," it was surely necessary to offer branch banking throughout Trinidad and Tobago. Additionally, other banks had a head start of many, many years. There were already existing over 100 bank branches of the international banks.

Detractors also felt that too much money financing bank branches was being tied up in capital expenditure, instead of being used to provide loans and generate more profits. What they clearly missed was that when the bank rented premises, a situation was often created that worked against the bank. The rented location was enhanced by the bank's presence, and over time the landlord could raise the rent to unconscionable levels.

There was the experience of Barclays Bank (now Republic Bank) when it rented premises in the prestigious Salvatori Building in downtown Port of Spain. After establishing goodwill at the spot, Barclays found it necessary to close the branch, as high rental increases had become one of the negative factors.

Further, there was an issue of how NCB was financing the branch expansion. Banks have been known to make arrangements for a person to obtain property, then design and build to the specifications of the bank. The bank would then lend the money for construction, and the lease payment by the bank to the landlord would be sufficient for the bank's landlord to repay the ten to fifteen year loan. Ownership of the property would remain with the landlord on repayment of the mortgage, with the bank owning nothing and remaining tenants for life, with unknown possible rental increases.

While there may have been a few positives to it, the sad part about such an arrangement in a small society like Trinidad and Tobago was that it could become open to corruption. Insiders are favored since they know what locations the banks are interested in, and such transactions could end up not proceeding on a transparent and fair basis.

In support of our branch expansion plan, our management was able to establish that while short-term profits of NCB might have been reduced, this was more than compensated for by medium and long-term profits—thanks to the savings in escalating rent. Additionally, the real estate of the branches experienced tremendous long-term capital appreciation. This last particular assertion was later borne out by the capital reserves which were available from NCB to the successor First Citizens Bank—real estate values of the properties of NCB had increased, in some cases, more than ten to fifteen times of the original purchase price.

Another dimension to branch expansion

Bank branches needed competent persons to manage the operations and employees. NCB'S recruitment and training strategies provided the answers. The branch network represents the sinews that make the banking operations available to a wide cross-section of society

The Branch Manager therefore played an important part in leading the success of NCB. In 1985, Mr. Melville P. Lewis and Mr. Maurice Gonsalves were appointed the first Regional Managers being responsible for seven and six branches respectively. In the life of NCB several persons were appointed Branch Managers (see Interface, Volume 3 1985) and some of these branch managers are:

Mr. Alphie Skerrette, Mr. Bertram Clarke, Ms. Veronica Simon, Ms. Donna Romilly, Mr. Henckle Lall, Ms. Vashti Chariah, Mr. Selwyn Berment, Ms. Marian Leavitt, Mr. Winston Rajah, Mrs. Jeanette La Barrie, Mr. Afza Mohammed, Mrs. Josephine Charles, Mr. Mc Donald Rodney, Mrs. Annabelle Mohammed, Ms. Kimlan Wong, Mr. Jim Mykoo, Mr. Lennox Koylass, Ms. Jean Alexander, Mr.

Lionel Seunarine, Mrs. Priscilla Peters, Mr. Cuthbert Alleyne, Mr. Mario Young, Ms. Sanjean Thomas, Ms. Anushka Recile, Mrs. Ligia Farnum, Ms. Angela Alexander, Mrs. Susan Jacobs, Mr. Denis Mouttet, Mrs. Audrey Gomes, Mr. Kenrick Seegobin, Mr. Egbert Lewis, Mrs. Laura Cozier, Mrs. Patricia Mosca, Mrs. Judy Wood Solomon, Mr. Norman Chang, Mr. Edwin Chariah, Mr. Vishnu Gajadhar, Mrs. Deanna Allamani, Ms. Margo Charles, and Ms. Valerie Lee Chong

Run Silent, Run Deep

There were many employees who were not overly assertive, but gave effective valiant service in promoting the success of NCB. Some of these staff members were: Ms. Maxine Charles, Mr. Michael Bazzie, Mr. Denis Ramdeen, Mr. Brian D'Abreau, Mr. Gregory Bissessar, Ms. Angela Gabriel, Mr. Lalchan Mahabir, Mrs. Zena Paul, Ms. Zora Ali, Mr. David Thompson, Mrs. Trixie Guy, Mr. Roger Ho Sing, Mrs. Bernice Cheung, Mr. Ivan Farinha, Mrs. Donna Latiff, Mrs. Susan Awai-Crichlow, Ms. Helen Pierre, Mr. Sean Corbie, Mr. Derek Walcott, Mr. Peter Neckles, Miss Patricia Mc.Kenzie, Mr. Micheson Neptune, Ms. Audrey Hernandez, Mrs. Janet Bishop-Lewis, Ms. Angela Charles, Mrs.

Marie Chai Hong, Mrs. Jennyln Branker, Mrs. Christina Rodriguez, and Ms. Pat Whittle.

Without its Service Staff operating effectively, NCB could not fulfill its mandate. Thus, special thanks are in order for the various couriers, messengers, cleaners, chauffeurs, maids, security officers, and all other such employees. *AN INDIVIDUAL BY HIMSELF/HERSELF, CAN SELDOM ACHIEVE ANYTHING OF GREAT SIGNIFICANCE. THE INDIVIDUAL, HOWEVER, CAN ACCOMPLISH MUCH BY ENLISTING THE SUPPORT OF THE MANY OTHER PERSONS WHO ARE THE PIECES IN THE PUZZLE OF A PARTICULAR ACHIEVEMENT. THUS, THE AUTHOR HAS RAISED THE HANDS OF MANY, NOT ALL, OF THE PERSONS WHO WERE PART OF THE PUZZLE OF NCB'S SUCCESS.*

Tobago Operations

To be faithful to its name, "National Commercial Bank of Trinidad and Tobago," a branch of NCB was necessary to be established in Tobago. In the ninth Annual Report of NCB at page 6 is stated:

"It is expected that the branch expansion will mushroom in the next two years, when an additional eight branches will come on stream. We will then have a reasonable network of sixteen branches. The most significant and strategic of these is the branch of the National Commercial Bank in Scarborough, Tobago. This establishment of a physical presence in Tobago will be a major achievement."

This was followed up in the Twelfth Annual Report of NCB at page 3 as follows:

"A special word about our operations in Tobago. Our establishment in Tobago has been as successful as the Trinidad operations. We are the only Bank to have 2 outlets in Tobago even though we were the last of 6 banks to establish there. Moreover, the NCB is the only bank in Tobago established outside the capital of Scarborough. The Scarborough Branch is already profitable although it was only opened in January 1980.

The outlet in Roxborough that opened in December 1981 has met our expectations. The decision to have 2 outlets in Tobago was a sound one."

Bank competence

The marketing strategies of the bank had to deal with the main concerns of potential customers: these were **CONFIDENTIALTY, CONVENIENCE, AND COMPETENCE.** In carrying out this mandate, the foundation was truth in advertising, and strict validity of information in the content of media releases.

Overarching the three Cs are being a good corporate citizen and having a social responsibility outreach in various communities. The usual media platforms were used but designed to be distinguishable from the marketing strategies of the competitive international commercial banks.

Persons needed to know that their money was entrusted to persons of competence who will safeguard their money. The first requirement was to appoint managerial staff that could be compared positively to the staff of the international banks operating in Trinidad and Tobago. This was relatively easy as there were numerous local persons who had been University trained through Government scholarships or their own initiative.

These new management recruits then integrated with their communities and became community thought leaders. They were involved in community projects that established their profiles. One example of this was that the Chief Executive of NCB hosted an educational radio series on Money and Banking. This program comprised one hundred and four 4-minute programs on all aspects of money and banking. Some of the topics were deposits, loans, treasury bills, Caribbean Development Bank, foreign exchange, International Monetary Fund, travelers' cheques, Central Bank, and Government Bonds. This had a tremendous impact, as the customers of other banks started to visit the National Commercial Bank to enquire whether their banks were being fair to them.

Of course, the proof of the pudding is in the eating, so that the Bank's internal systems had to allow the staff to deliver competent service when customers and potential customers visited the bank. Moreover, staff had to have the technical competence of commercial banking and be customer savvy—hence the NCB'S preoccupation with training of staff.

Better facilitation for small and medium business loans

There was a major gap in our country's financing profile before the birth of the National Commercial Bank. There existed a negative bias of the existing commercial banks' *financing of new and inexperienced local businesses.* This could be expected since two critical loan criteria—a successful business history and appropriate security to qualify for a business loan—would have been deficient in many new local enterprises.

The challenge of NCB was to be somewhat more flexible than the foreign banks, while maintaining its responsibilities of fiduciary trust for its depositors, and profitability for its shareholders. It will be instructive to reflect on some of the finance "traps" that faced our new breed of budding businessmen.

Business Failure Rate

In the 1970's eight out of every ten businesses in the United States of America *failed within their first five years.* There was no comparative research done for businesses in Trinidad and Tobago, but NCB'S suspicion was that the statistics were not much different in Trinidad and Tobago. Why was there such a failure rate?

Research in the United States concluded that those businesses were simply opening their doors for the wrong reasons: they were not businesses; they were jobs! NCB'S own historical observations in the case of Trinidad and Tobago confirmed this view.

For example, there was a master baker who came to NCB. He wanted to start his own business because he felt that he was working too hard for someone else. A year after he set up his business, he lamented to the bank that he was now working more hours than he did before. To become successful he had to shift from being self-employed, to establishing systems and employing others to do some of the tasks he had done himself previously.

The bank realized that the main reason for start-up business failure was the misconception that an owner was a self-employer rather than an entrepreneur. Thus, NCB'S edict to new business entrants was that *quality of life* should be considered important, and not merely *owning a business*. Business should be approached, the bank advised, as a route to a better life for the owner.

Thus, one needed to know what life he or she had already, and determine what better life he or she wanted the business to lead to. If the business were merely an opportunity to be self-employed, it was hardly likely that the business would afford the owner a better life. Those people might instead end up being slaves to their businesses with no quality time to enjoy life, while also damaging their health and perhaps losing their families in the process.

The question of the times was, *"What makes a business succeed?"* The answer has always been *a clear purpose for the business, effective employees, and systems that deliver that purpose with cost-effectiveness.* If the purpose is principally to be your own boss, or to use your technical skills for your own reward rather than hire those capabilities out, you are not really growing a business. Most of the new breed of business owners did not clarify the purposes of their businesses and did not institute systems to deliver those purposes.

Whether it is a bank, a McDonald's franchise, a telecommunications company, or a small start-up enterprise, its success and growth depend on rigorous implementation of systems. The current system must be observed, and there must be a procedure for the system to be changed in response to new circumstances. When there is a change in the system, everyone concerned must know and follow it.

Closely observing the struggles that investors were undergoing, NCB developed ten reasons why new Trinidad & Tobago businesses failed. Before sharing these, consider five common finance traps that have caused many start-up businesses in Trinidad and Tobago to flounder.

The Five Finance Traps

The first trap is the absence of adequate financing for the business. When a person is thinking about getting a business off the ground, he or she obviously must have a good idea—*on* the ground!—of what product or service will be offered. The challenge specifically is to organize the various elements to deliver the commodity or service to the marketplace at the right time, in the right manner, at the right price, and with consistently good quality. There has to be an integration of the *location* at which the business will operate, the *machinery* and *tools* necessary for production, *raw materials*, *stock*, and the *personnel* to man the operations.

Fitting all these pieces together require *money* for its financing, and this was the first finance trap that beset these new business owners. Quite often there was not sufficient funding to do properly all that was needed. The business started undercapitalized; thus from the outset it was financially and operationally disadvantaged. Usually, this got appreciably worse as time progressed.

The start-up owner looked to the financial institutions for help, but—regrettably for the owner— the policies of financial institutions did not easily assist entrepreneurs to get their much-needed funds. Banks' institutional policies required strict security and a history of successful performance in the business—two elements that most indigenous start-up owners did not have. Also, the legal banking statutory framework mandates strict guidelines in the areas of security and risk.

New business-owners who have their request turned down tend to be angry, as they argue indignantly that, if they had the money, they would not need the bank. Of course, notwithstanding such an understandable, emotional viewpoint, the bank has to ensure that each borrower has a sufficient financial stake in the business, so that both the bank and the owner shoulder the risk by sharing in it. There was an NCB customer who was highly annoyed that the bank did not finance her great creative idea to establish a boutique. She had no savings or other assets to introduce into the business, to reflect her risk and confidence in the enterprise, so the bank declined the business loan.

The second finance trap arose when the unexpected happened—any unforeseen development that would put the business in deep financial jeopardy; for example, delinquent customers or spoiled materials or imperfect finished goods. One measure that could have helped was the partnering of two or more budding business entrepreneurs rather than business adventurers trying to make it individually. The bigger the business goal, the greater is the necessity to network financially.

Partnerships and joint shareholding have their own special problems, but those can be at times the least of the demons for many start-up owners. And partners need not all put in *money*. One may provide funds, another the business location, and yet another personal services, but these must be clearly spelt out in s Shareholders' Agreement. The culture often witnessed by the bank was generally one of "Lone Rangers." The majority of people were reluctant to give up their individual business independence.

An unusual example of this type of cooperation was the case of three advertising executives who joined forces to form their own advertising agency. One was the accountant; the second, the creative director; and the third, a copywriter. Their company did quite well, and some years later merged with a successful larger advertising agency.

The third finance trap occurred when the business was successful and the owner, in error, mistook cash for profits. The business would show a daily healthy cash flow, and the owner would think, *This is my business. I account to no one. I took the risk and put in my money to establish the business ... I am entitled to take from the till whatever I want.* That sort of thinking was disastrous. In most instances, not even a definite weekly or monthly amount was established thus leading to withdrawals in excess of profits: cash in the register is not necessarily profits, as among other things, goods sold have to be replenished from cash in the register. Many good companies failed because funds that should have been *reinvested* to maintain and grow the business were withdrawn by the owner for spending *outside* the business. Over time, this cash drain came to mean that depleted stocks could not be replaced. Sales would at best decline, eventually drying up altogether, and the business would ultimately collapse. An associated aspect was demands made by family members and close friends of the owner. They also did not understand that withdrawing cash improperly from a business would quickly kill the goose that was laying the golden eggs.

NCB once dealt with a customer who had a thriving business importing mainly dairy products, and the bank could not understand how his overdraft was always up to the limit. Investigations revealed that he was taking cash from the business to buy personal assets not connected with the business. He did not understand that the heavy flow of cash was not profit. He needed some of that money to provide for restocking.

The fourth finance trap was the belief that the business could not afford to pay to design a proper accounting system or at least arrange to have monthly and quarterly financial statements available soon after the respective periods had ended. Without regular financial statements, owners and operators could not know the true condition of their businesses. Thus, they would not be aware of the need to, for instance, adopt new strategies in sufficient time to turn around the misfortunes of their businesses.

There was one customer, a financial services company, that appeared to be doing quite well but could not produce its final accounts. When NCB insisted on the audit to continue its line of credit, it was discovered that employees of the firm had defrauded the company of several hundred thousand dollars, causing the firm to collapse. Monthly management accounts produced on a timely and regular basis might have exposed the fraud much earlier and saved the company from extinction.

The fifth finance trap was old-fashioned greed or, put another way, an excessive drive to maximize profits. A business might have been quite successful at an early stage of its life and at a particular level. However, to increase the scale of operations to make more profits, without first increasing the finances to support such a surge could prove suicidal.

Another example was a business doubling its normal order of imported raw materials in anticipation of a change in the exchange rate. With no matching change in production and sales cycles, the cash flow began to creak under the strain. It became difficult to satisfy creditors, and soon the business came crashing down the slippery slope on which it had been unwittingly placed.

From working with hundreds of start-up enterprises, NCB identified the following top ten factors for failure:

1. Lack of management systems
2. Lack of vision and purpose of principals
3. Lack of financial planning and review
4. Over-dependence on specific individuals in the business
5. Poor market segmentation and strategy
6. Failure to establish and communicate company goals
7. Lack of knowledge about the market and the competition

8. Inadequate working capital or lack of funds
9. Absence of a standardized quality program
10. Owner concentrating on technical rather than strategic issues.

Financial Advisor

Whenever the bank undertook the role of financial advisor, its greatest intervention was to bring about a shift in the corporate thinking of the new breed of owners. The major platform was that fiscal success required the operations to have innovation, quantification, and orchestration. The business must embrace *innovation* to meet the changing dynamics; it must have *quantification* in all areas of activity since "what gets measured gets done"; and there must be *orchestration* in order to eliminate whimsical choice at the operational level. (In the last two, the operational mantra was that it was permissible to be *ruthless* in your correctness but not advisable to be *rootless* in your choices.)

NCB also discerned that there must be systems throughout the business to tell how things are to be done—from recruiting to answering the telephone, from tidying up to structured training, and from disciplining to dialoguing. There must be systems that tell how to manage the business, and there must be systems to tell how to change any of the procedures to ensure the company remains on top of its game.

This may be the Information Age, but it is quickly being superseded by the *Imagination* Age. Whatever you imagine, formulate, or truly believe, and relevantly act upon massively you can achieve. You may be your own boss, but you must be more than that. You must be an entrepreneur. You must develop methods for your enterprise that permit it to run on a day-by-day basis without your having to be physically there continuously throughout the day to do the work. This can be achieved by focusing on developing systems that tell your people how to perform. You'll be training people to do work and not have to depend on duplicating yourself for the business to grow.

Remember, an organism either grows or it dies, it cannot remain static for too long. A business is much the same.

Gender neglect in the case of females

There were three areas in which females were not treated properly:

(a) Their income was not taken into account for mortgage financing

(b) Products were not specifically designed to attract women

(c) Women were not given due recognition in businesses for management positions

In Trinidad and Tobago in 1970, banking policy did not accept joining the income of a woman to her husband's income for determining the income threshold of the family's finances. Additionally, as a matter of policy, women were not given mortgages in their own individual capacity. It did not matter whether the woman was a doctor, lawyer, accountant or other professional.

The income solution

NCB introduced a two-prong policy that covered professional and non-professional women. The basic concern was whether the women had a reasonable possibility that their earning capacity was likely to continue during the life of the mortgage loan. If you were a professional woman, your income qualified to be used for mortgage purposes. If you were a non-professional woman your income qualified, if you were in permanent paid employment for at least 5 years and your credit rating otherwise was of a good standing.

Relevant products

NCB'S review of banking products showed that women were not specifically targeted for business although they formed such a critical element in the economy. Historically, women managed the house and had a great influence on expenditure of the household.

In an article in the Express in a Supplement on page 21 headlined **"NCB PUTS SPOTLIGHT ON WOMEN"** the commentary in the article was as follows:

"The advertisements reflect women in various situations. Some are students, some are career women, some are housewives, some are young, but in all of them the message is the same—financial independence is important, especially for women.

"The advertisements referred to here are part of the campaign done by the National Commercial Bank (NCB) for its new Chaconia Savings Plan. They were deliberately designed to appeal directly to women. Explaining this was Philip Rochford, Chairman/Managing Director of NCB.

"Female critics of the campaign have asked: "Why women, and why not men? Rochford noted first of all that it was not a discriminatory tactic.

As a matter of fact, men are saving on the plan but NCB wanted to appeal directly to women because traditionally women have always been good money managers, even when they have not been financially independent.

"Rochford explained that when the bank was looking at ideas for the campaign, one consideration was that the bank should deal with an area that had potential, but had not been encouraged to develop that potential.

"We looked at it from the historical and subjective and then from an objective verifiable view. We concluded that women have always been central to the growth of the economy of the family, whether or not she was working, and that women have always had a heavy say in what happens to the home finances.

"Historically the woman has always optimized money. She has always been a keen manager of the finances of the home. 'The point of optimization is important' Rochford said 'because no matter how small the income is to run the home, whether she is single or married, the woman has always been able to save money.'

"And you can bet anything that when the family is in trouble, there is a nest egg saved by the woman in the home for the hard times." Rochford said.

"But the fiscal aptness of woman is not something that has always been appreciated. Although women have always been on the road to optimizing finances, it has not always been encouraged or articulated.

"The percentage of working women in the population to non-working women is another aspect of the women's market at which NCB looked. The 1980 population census showed that there was a working population of 466,800. Of this figure women totaled 156,800; that is a percentage of 33.6. From this we estimated that there were probably 190,000 females over the age of 21 who are not working. But bearing in mind that non-working women who are managing homes do have a tremendous influence on the disposition of funds, it was felt that here is a powerful market source.

"Rochford explained that the advertisements are really meant to sensitize women to continued fiscal awareness. It is perhaps pertinent that while there has always been the onus on women in the home to manage the family's money, there are growing numbers of women who are discovering the importance of financial independence as a reality. A large percentage of these are women who are divorced with families.

"Beating his chest a little Rochford said, that

"while there are other banks which have been in the business longer than NCB and that all banks offer, basically the same services, none of them have ever made an appeal to this critical group in society."

"But the Bank's message is not simply women must save. This is just one aspect. For example, while it has been low key, we have been actively supporting all women's groups in their various areas of activity, so that as a group women will become a more positive force.

"Women can have a tremendous impact on the growth of savings and the growth of investment in the economy. This must lead to an improvement in the quality of life. Basically we hope that our campaign will trigger women to become more intense about their plans for the future."

Women in Bank Management

When NCB was launched in 1970, there were more females than males working in the various commercial banks. However, there was a dearth of women in managerial positions. In the case of NCB there were several women who had significant experience and career loyalty to be trained and prepared for management positions. In fact, Mrs. Annette De Silva was NCB'S First Female Branch

Manager. NCB'S second Branch was opened in Arima, Trinidad, and eventually Mrs. De Silva was appointed its Branch Manager. There was no gender discrimination at NCB, and preferment was based on skills, training, experience and efficiency in relation to the job to be done.

Emphasis on female managerial appointments was advertised in the media telling the story of their progress, and this had a demonstration effect on organizations beyond the banking sector.

New elements

There were subtle but significant interventions that helped to develop the structure of the society, and these are some of them.

Local orientation

The fact that NCB was an indigenous bank was a distinction that had positive effects for persons with a national consciousness. However, the bank wanted persons to choose the bank because of its relevance and efficacy. Thus our promotions and advertisements did not overtly promote that it was a local bank. The approach was to engage in activities and with a voice that demonstrated NCB'S local orientation. For example, the models in the advertisements were also clearly of local origin.

Play of the Month

There were many good playwrights producing several wonderful plays, but they did not get sponsorship or sufficient exposure. A mitigating factor was that the local plays were much more expensive to produce than buying foreign canned television programs. NCB sponsored one play each month—The Play of the Month—provided a person from Trinidad and Tobago produced the play, and that it had not been previously shown on television. Later on, the playwright producer was extended to include Playwrights from other Caribbean Countries.

Sponsorship

The international banks supported sports and cultural activities, but there was a niche not being served. Clubs that were not in top positions in their fields, and clubs that were located in rural areas, and sports that were not particularly popular in the public domain were neglected in sponsorship. NCB supported these neglected areas.

Chess

An interesting effort was NCB'S attempt to assist in sharpening the minds of the citizenry by exposing them to the game of chess. A chessboard was provided in the newspapers, and the reader would only have to cut it out and paste it onto a bit of cardboard—and *voila!*—a bona fide Chess Board for his or her first game. The various chess pieces were beautifully designed by one of our then agency heads Mr. Jerry Besson (then more of an artist and now more of a historian). Chess Pieces were designed and could be cut out of the newspapers and glued to soft drinks' bottle caps. This provided the Chess pieces.

The bank sponsored a series of radio programs in which Mr.Frank Brassington, local chess master, was commissioned to teach listeners to play chess. At the end of that series, the bank produced an instructional booklet and made it available free of charge. This generated great interest in chess and spawned many chess players in Trinidad and Tobago.

But why choose chess? Chess is a game that promotes critical thinking, which is key for personal development and nation building.

Chess is a good representation of maneuvers in life. You play against someone, your goal being to get your opponent into a position where his or her king cannot be moved without entering a space on the board that you control. That was "checkmate" for the king, thus ending the game and making you the winner.

Different pieces on the board can be moved in different directions, just as life presents different choices. Each player has to anticipate the other player's actions at least two to three moves ahead of every play. Anticipation is one of the signs of true wisdom. Moreover, players suffer the losses or enjoy the benefits from the choices they make. These factors, among others, would develop the thinking skills of players.

The Bank saw all of this as healthy exercise for a population both young and yearning for development. The minds of our future generations, indeed our future leaders, would be helped by a collective intellect that went deeper and further than the minds of our predecessors. This critical thinking would help to take charge of our nation's destiny, pulling us up creatively and managing our affairs uniquely.

Trinidad and Tobago would then hope to interact with more developed countries with confidence, courage, and civilized conquest. The provision of chess was but one humble step in the Bank's contribution to the progress of Trinidad and Tobago, and it was well within the parameters of an institution such as ours. The initials NCB had as one of its meanings, *Nationals Conquering Banking*!

NCB was moving in a continuous cycle of learning, teaching, following, and leading. It was at the same time turning out to be one of the core reasons for the excitement experienced within the bank and the buzz across Trinidad and Tobago. Later generations would say that NCB was becoming "hot" (or "cool," depending on the particular generation). Naturally enough, the Bank was starting to attract different kinds of attention.

Conversing with history

Conversing with History was a Sunday afternoon one hour radio program where senior media practitioners interviewed persons who contributed significantly to some aspect of the development of Trinidad and Tobago. The purpose was twofold; to tell the story of success to let others know what was possible, and to instruct and inspire others to pursue their own dreams. When their life stories were analyzed, some values that were common to all these achievers were: clarity of vision, commitment, persistence, massive relevant action, keeping up to date in their respective fields, contribution beyond narrow personal benefit, belief in oneself, and gratitude for personal blessings. Unfortunately, these recordings were lost in the archives.

Some of these success achievers were:

Sir Solomon Hochoy, Sir Ellis Clark, Dr. Patrick Solomon, Mr. Roy Joseph, Ms. Dolly Beckles, Mr. Clifford Roach, Mr. Jeffrey Stollmeyer, Ms. Beryl McBurnie, Mr. Patrick Chookolingo, Brigadier Joffre C. Serrette, Mr.Winston 'Spree' Simon, Ms. Anna Mahase, Mr. Albert Gomes, Mr. Tubal Uriah 'Buzz' Butler, Mr. Patrick Castagne, Mr. Thomas Gatcliffe, Professor Lloyd Braithwaite, Mr. Cyril Duprey, Mr. Carlyle Chang, and Mr.Andrew Carr.

Mrs. Barbara Sankar, Manager Public Relations and Marketing, Ms. Janice Bodden, Mrs. Elizabeth Millar, and Mrs. Insie Jasmine King-Toney who kept the secretarial, communication, and public relations circle of the Managing Director's Office were loyal competent, confidential and communication sensitive, and are owed a special debt of gratitude for NCB'S success.

Special tribute must be paid to Mr. Alfred Aguiton and Ms. Astra da Costa, then Joint Owners of All Media Projects Limited (AMPLE) for their exquisite and faithful rendition of NCB'S advertising and public relations creative outreach. Special thanks are also in order for the contribution of Creative Advertising Limited.

Public Speaking

It was clear that the Managers of NCB as Ambassadors of the Bank had to be able to tell the story of the bank in an effective voice. While citizens of Trinidad and Tobago are natural talkers they need to be polished to the level of international standards of Public Speaking. Having reviewed the various options available, the conclusion was that Toastmasters International would best meet the needs of the bank and at the same time, also the general public. The Bank therefore sent away for a kit to become familiar with what was required to establish Toastmasters' Clubs.

When a great idea is released in the Universe, usually several minds simultaneously connect to it. The outcome of the idea depends on the manner in which it is thought through and the commitment and persistence of the thinking of the persons to whom the idea occurred.

It was therefore a delight when two members of staff of the then National Commercial Bank of Trinidad and Tobago Limited quite independently raised the possibility of introducing Toastmasters to the Bank. One person was Mr. Nazeer Sultan, who became the Club's first President and later achieved being an Able Toastmaster Bronze. The other initiator, Mr. Courtney Garcia, eventually returned to Canada where he had studied. The rest is history.

Two Clubs were formed: The National Commercial Bank Toastmasters Club and The NCB Sports Toastmasters Club. The former became defunct when NCB was merged as part of First Citizens Bank. The latter changed its name to the Dynamic Toastmasters Club.

There were two phases contemplated. First, the Managers, their staff and their spouses would be given the opportunity to become 'Leaders as Learners' by being eligible for membership in the first two Toastmasters Clubs. The second phase would be to have numerous clubs activated throughout Trinidad and Tobago by the demonstration effect of the first two NCB Toastmasters Clubs.

Toastmasters' philosophy is that the skill of doing comes from doing. Thus, at all Club meetings the emphasis is on everyone in the meeting participating in some manner. This participation is extended to the guests who are given an opportunity to speak themselves at the end of the meeting: they have the possibility of giving feedback on their impressions of the proceedings

The Toastmasters message is simple. Each person can continually improve his/her speaking ability by following a tested structure, continuous speaking practice and tender nurturing and support by other Toastmasters, through effective evaluation of their speaking. Besides this educational component of Toastmasters meetings, Toastmasters provides training in the business side of meetings and in team building.

Individuals normally speak around two years of age. In fact, the research shows that on average a person speaks sufficient words in one year to fill at least one book of 300 pages. However, the issue is whether an individual is getting the desired results from each communication that is made.

Communicate or be stunted. This is the challenge of personal growth. A person who keeps all his/her thoughts, ideas and values to himself/herself will die as a person. He/she has to make the thoughts known. The thoughts have to leave the privacy of the mind and be expressed. At a fundamental level the thoughts become public when they are released from the private domain of the mind. The 'public' may be just one other person, a group, a large audience or the entire Country. The promise of Toastmasters is to help the individual to become a better communicator. The individual will then be more effective in his/her creative expression.

A survey of Toastmasters was conducted in the Philippines, Australia, New Zealand, California, South Dakota and Idaho to find out how the Toastmasters Program had helped the individuals. The overwhelming response was confidence - confidence to speak before a group clearly, concisely and with empathy. Similarly, in Trinidad and Tobago, the members of its Toastmasters' Clubs have made great advances.

Public speaking is powerful. It is important, as it is the vehicle by which a person influences his or her acquaintances, friends, families, workplace, immediate environment and the wider community.

Therefore, you must resolve today to build an arsenal of skills, techniques and tools to get your desired results from every communication that you make. You can commit to your own self-improvement public speaking program or you can enroll as a member in Toastmasters International. Be steadfast, think, act and be, to bring more meaning to your life. Be the best that you can be through skills training of being a better communicator.

Your quality of life depends on the quality of your personal relationships, and successful personal relationships depend on effective communications. What you will learn and the results you will achieve as a Toastmaster are nothing compared to what you will become from being a Toastmaster. Become the Master Communicator that you have the potential of becoming. Become a more active Toastmaster and soar as an eagle. Join the family of Toastmasters and be part of PEOPLE BUILDING PEOPLE. *At the time of writing this book, there are nine Toastmasters' Clubs in Trinidad and one in Tobago.*

Operational synchrony between all commercial banks

NCB concluded after due research and investigation, it would be in the interests of the banks, as well as the Country, if the banks co-operated in the use of their Automated Business Machines (ABM).

The idea was to develop an operational technological system in which a customer of one bank could transact business with another bank through the use of an ABM Linx System that interconnected all banks. To accomplish this, the banks had to agree and become the shareholders of the technological company that would carry out the policies of the banks in that regard.

Originally, the banks did not agree, as this appeared to go counter to their individual competitive stance. NCB persisted and with one other bank and a financial entity, incorporated a company and started the process. Eventually good sense prevailed and all the commercial banks joined in the ABM Linx System. The project was successfully led and implemented through Mr. Andrew Mc Eachrane, NCB'S Deputy Managing Director and Chief Operating Officer. The result is that now a customer from one bank can access his account through another bank using a plastic card integrated with the ABM Linx System. It would have been a waste of resources, and perhaps inoperative, if each bank attempted implementing its own separate solution of interbank cash transactions.

National Political Support

One operational objective was that the bank should be a National Institution, notwithstanding that it was originally 100% Government owned. The vision was that all political parties and significant interest groups should feel comfortable banking at the National Bank, irrespective of their political affiliation. This objective was achieved as at one time all the major political parties banked at NCB.

Hon. Bhadase Sagan Maraj

Just before the NCB was opened there was discussion on it in the House of Representatives, and Hon. Bhadase Maraj, then Opposition Member for Chaguanas lodged a cheque for $25,000 with Mr. George Chambers, Minister of State in the Ministry of Finance, for safe keeping to be deposited when the new bank opened for business on July 01.

Mr. Maraj advised that the cheque showed his good faith in the Country and assured the Minister that the Opposition supported this bank 100%.

Hon. Basdeo Panday

During one of the Campaigns of a General Election there was a meeting at the University of Woodford Square at which Hon. Basdeo Panday, then Political Leader of the United National Congress, and Leader of the Opposition encouraged the audience to bank at the National Commercial Bank. He advised that he had moved his account to the High Street, San Fernando Branch of NCB; and in fact, the Manager of this San Fernando NCB Branch, Mr. Ganace

Ramdial, was present in the audience. There was immediate tremendous applause by the audience.

National Joint Action Committee (NJAC)

The Express Newspapers of 25 June 1986 at page 6, the headline was **"NJAC praises Rochford."** The article stated as follows: "The National Joint Action Committee (NJAC) has praised National Commercial Bank (NCB) Chairman Philip Rochford for his "enlightened approach" to the banking sector.

"NJAC was referring specifically to Rochford's statements that the banking sector as a whole could take a more enlightened approach to help their customers in these difficult times by reducing rates, cutting back charges and rescheduling debts as banks did in Canada during the early eighties.

"NJAC was praising Rochford's statements in the light of what it saw as the general feeling that with the loss of the "all important oil revenues", the nation was being "deluded" into thinking that the IMF type of solutions were the prescription for our woes.

"NJAC quoted from present issues of its newspapers. *The Liberation* which said the People's National Movement (PNM) government had "willingly adopted practices and concepts laid down by the international institutions without consideration of our own peculiarities and without consulting the nation."

"NJAC had expressed "disappointment" with the private sector whom, it thought, had fallen into the same pattern.

"But while praising Rochford for "his realistic approach to the financial state" of the country, NJAC said it was "uncomfortable that as an eminent financier Mr. Rochford needs to take his cue from Canada to deal with our problems when it is well documented that NJAC has been consistently calling for the same attitude based on a rational assessment of the local situation."

"In the release NJAC said it had always been for the full utilization of our nation's intellectual resources, both academic and non-academic, to ensure that we can steer our own path to economic development.

"Had this been followed, the party stated, a decade and a half ago, "the fundamental errors of financial management" that occurred during the boom period would never have been."

Hon. Trevor Sudama

A Newspaper article on 15 April 1987 headlined "SUDAMA CHALLENGES NCB" goes on to comment as follows: "Minister in the Ministry of Finance, Trevor Sudama questioned whether the National Commercial Bank (NCB) had achieved its aspirations and expectations and challenged the bank to re-assess its objectives.

"Sudama was on Saturday evening opening the Point Lisas Branch of NCB. The Minister reviewed the objectives of the bank. He said: 'Perhaps more than any other, it was established to fulfill the aspirations of the government and people of Trinidad and Tobago for the attainment of a significant degree of control over our domestic finances and to ensure the mobilization of such resources into the productive sectors of the economy.'

"Said Sudama: 'Such aspirations and expectations remain valid today as they ever were, and one may now ask for some kind of assessment as to the achievement of that objective which was set some time ago'. Sudama said: 'The government recognized the difficulties faced by the bank over the years, including the competition from the larger and more established banks'. He said that: 'The NCB had overcome the problems and now had a market share of 15 per cent of deposits in the banking industry and 15 per cent of the industry's loans market; this compared with less than 2 per cent market share in 1971." He said, "the paid up capital of the bank increased from $5 million in 1971 to $31 million in 1986 and there were over 20,000 shareholders.'

"He said the bank serviced over 100,000 customers or about one fifth of the working population; the assets of the bank grew from $23 million in 1971 to $1.8 billion in 1986 and the bank had shown a profit every year. He said the bank had received tremendous support from the government and the public and described these as notable achievements and a demonstration of the capacity of nationals to manage financial institutions."

"Said Sudama: 'Notwithstanding these achievements there seems to persist a viewpoint that the NCB should have been more aggressive in pioneering new and innovative methods which were more development oriented rather than the traditional commercial banking.'

"He said: 'The bank had now captured the confidence of the people and a sizable portion of the market and was now in a position to influence the banking sector.'

"He said: 'The government expects NCB to properly fulfill the aspirations which informed and motivated its establishment."

CHAPTER 6

PROJECTS THAT DID NOT FULLY MATERIALIZE

Sole Agency for foreign payments overseas

Commissions and rates charged by commercial banks for making foreign payments overseas represent an important part of the income of commercial banks. NCB saw this as a strategic area to take monopoly control for the benefit of Trinidad and Tobago, including monitoring, at that time, the relatively scarce foreign reserves of the Country.

The proposition by NCB to the Government of Trinidad and Tobago was that legislation be enacted to authorize NCB as the Authority to make all foreign exchange payments from Trinidad and Tobago. The legislation would provide for NCB to appoint all commercial banks as NCB'S sub-agents for this purpose.

This arrangement would not interfere with

customers of other banks doing their ordinary banking business. The sub-agents would get a percentage commission for each transaction and NCB would receive a commission on every foreign exchange transaction: this would amount to sizable income for NCB and redound to the benefit of the citizenry of Trinidad and Tobago.

The proposal was not a novel one. At that time in the early life of NCB similar approaches were being considered in the Countries of Chile and Peru. This revolutionary idea for Trinidad and Tobago was not accepted and developed. It may be that then there was such a strong lobby of the international banks that their citadel could not be penetrated.

Interest payments on large checking account balances

In 1970, as a matter of policy, commercial banks did not pay interest on checking account balances. NCB saw this as a marketing opening. State Enterprises and other public bodies who normally held large credit balances were targeted.

The enterprises were delighted that there was a hidden source of income available to the institutions, and several of them agreed to transfer their business to NCB. However, under the Exchequer and Audit Ordinance the Minister of Finance had to give approval for the transfer of the banking account.

There was a notable priority case where the enterprise over the years held millions of dollars in free balances in its checking account. When the enterprise's bank was advised why the account was being moved to NCB, an offer was made by their bank to match NCB'S offer to make interest payments on their large credit balances. The Board of the enterprise countered that it was "too little, too late".

However, the enterprise's bank advised the Minister of Finance that if the account were moved, the bank would call in the loans and overdrafts of the Government of Trinidad and Tobago, as was the bank's entitlement under the legal terms of the credit arrangements. The account was not transferred to NCB, but the enterprise was paid interest by its bank as proposed by NCB. In any event, the customer received a benefit not available previously, and many other customers benefitted by a new policy arrangement of paying interest on minimum large daily credit balances.

Disappointment

The communication efforts were not all successful. In "Business Information" Issue No 7 of 1986, the following is stated:

"We have completed sixteen issues (16) of our internal publication, "Business Information" and it is therefore timely to assess whether it has achieved its intended purpose. The primary purpose of the Business Information Bulletin was to permit the management group from Grade 6's to the Managing Director, an opportunity to express their views professionally on matters of interest and relevance to the business of the customers of the bank and of the bank itself. This opportunity was important since there was no similar publication available in our country to the management group.

"We had also hoped that the publication would be a channel for the management group to articulate their views and influence the environment. Of course, we expected that the fund of information would have provided a good cross-fertilization between the members of the management group and would have contributed to the advancement of knowledge and information in our society.

"Unfortunately, the record of contributions to the

publication is not encouraging. Only twenty-one (21) of a possible one hundred and eighty one (181) persons contributed to the publication. Moreover, the Managing Director contributed twelve (12) times, the Executive Assistant to the Managing Director six (6) times, five (5) other officers contributed twice each, and thirteen (13) other officers contributed one (1) article each. A further statistic shows that in the previous sixteen issues, no Branch Manager contributed, and neither of the two (2) General Managers contributed.

"In view of what appears to be a lack of interest generally by the members of the management group for whom the publication is intended, it is regretted that the publication will be suspended for the time being. If at a later stage, it appears that there is sufficient interest, the publication may be revived."

Signed: Philip G. Rochford, HBM
Managing Director
Editor-in-Chief

Audited Final Accounts

Experience in developed countries showed that, quite often, businesses that failed did not have up-to-date audited final accounts. This led NCB to devise a policy to facilitate audited accounts for the budding business class of the seventies, eighties, nineties, and onwards.

The final accounts of a firm are a helpful numerical representation of the effects of the policies, strategies, and practices of the firm. Thus, timely management accounts and audited accounts are key survival planks in good corporate architecture, infrastructure, and behavior. They provide early-warning signals of danger or of success.

The main constraint put forward by new or expanding businesses was that the audit fees were too expensive for them. NCB accepted this at face value, and as a result organized a panel of auditors from which the bank's clients could choose, with the bank paying the costs of the auditor. NCB assessed that if this policy saved each year three to four businesses—representing total outstanding loans of $1 million—from failing, the program would be self-financing for the bank. Moreover, this program would reduce the number of business failures.

There were many small and medium-sized accounting firms that made the audit fees competitive. The bank advertised for qualified accountants who wished to be on the panel. Strict criteria were established, including professional indemnity insurance for negligence. This panel opened up a new opportunity, especially for the more recently qualified local accountants.

However, there came yet another strange revelation; many customers did not take advantage of this offer for the bank to pay their audit fees! It was a phenomenon that led us to include a strict term of compliance for audited accounts in all new business loans and any renewals of existing credit facilities.

One of the bank's customers was very upset with this requirement. His business was doing quite well, but he wanted to diversify into an industry for which he had no experience. He requested that the bank loan him $15 million to acquire the new business.

The bank asked for the accounts of the prospective business for the last five years and his business plan. He had neither but became quite obnoxious, stating that his character should be sufficient. The $15 million loan was declined, and for a long time he was at odds with the Bank. Such was the expectation of some customers.

This program to assist businesses to secure their audited accounts was not as successful as the bank originally envisaged. What became obvious was that many of the businesses felt this strict oversight by the bank removed their flexibility to use the loans and proceeds of sales for non-business purposes. Not surprisingly, it was an attitude that led to many failures. On the other hand, those businesses that finessed their operations with the recommended professionalism profited greatly from it.

The Steel Pan Pilot Project

In its financial year 1987/88, NCB instituted a Steel Pan Pilot Project for a Soloist Pianist to play in the main banking hall of a bank branch from 3.00 p.m. to 5.00 p.m. every Friday afternoon for a stipulated stipend; this was a period during which there were very many customers in the bank. The bank's customers appreciated this musical serenading.

PAN TRINBAGO (Governing Body for Steel Bands throughout Trinidad and Tobago) was given the authority to administer the selection and deployment of the Soloist Panists and other administrative arrangements. The project started with selected Port of Spain branches of NCB.

The intention was that all the branches of NCB would eventually participate. The notion was that this idea would spread to all the commercial banks. If this occurred, as the banks had a total of over 100 branches, in the first instance, supplemental income would be provided for 300 to 400 Soloist Panists every month. Moreover, constant exposure would be given to the National Instrument, and other opportunities for the Pan Movement would arise.

This Pilot Project did not get full support for one reason and another. Apparently, it was an idea whose time had not yet come. A golden opportunity to elevate the National Instrument and bring more acclaim to steel band members was lost.

Banks' Rates and Charges

There was much public outcry in the United States of America, Canada and the United Kingdom for the high level of rates and charges imposed by their commercial banks. It was therefore strategic for NCB to take the initiative and pre-empt the situation In Trinidad and Tobago.

Accordingly, in 1986 Rates and Charges at NCB were adjusted downwards or eliminated. The Annual Report 1986/1987 of NCB stated 'inter alia' as follows on page 1:

"To assist our customers during the economic adjustment period our bank took several steps which could be summarized as follows:—

(i) Interest rates on loans were reduced while interest rates on deposits were either not changed or were reduced by smaller amounts than the changes in loan rates.

(ii) ***A number of rates and charges were abolished or reduced. . . . .***"

An expectation of NCB was that customers of other banks would put pressure on their banks to reduce rates or at least match the lower NCB'S levels. This did not happen. There were no significant changes and the customers of other banks accepted the continuing high rates and charges.

NCB analyzed the position and came to the following conclusions:

(i) The customer did not normally know the total cost of the individual customer's rates and charges. Where it was known, the amount was insignificant in relation to the total flow of funds in the customer's account.

(ii) While an individual charge may be unconscionable—say, $20.00 to get your own bank statement— such a statement was not regularly required, and so the customer did not rigorously fight the injustice.

(iii) Since all the other banks followed a similar pattern of rates and charges, moving between the other established banks did not solve the problem.

(iv) The level of rates and charges is not one of the principal reasons for a customer engaging to do business with a commercial bank.

New customer awareness

It appears that times are changing and customers are becoming more outraged at the injustice of inequitable rates and charges. The commercial banks are in a strong negotiating position in relation to their customers—take it or leave it. Perhaps the equalizing force should be the intervention of the Central Bank of Trinidad and Tobago that is the Statutory Regulator of the commercial banks

CARICOM Initiatives

The Bank's Annual Report 1980/81, stated 'inter alia,' ". . . NCB found itself involved in three (3) significant arrangements affecting the Caricom region. In the first place, we launched the Caricom Travelers' Cheques project in August 1980 to deal with the issue and encashment of Caricom Travelers' Cheques, negotiable only within the Caricom region.

One can safely describe this project as falling within the vision of NCB, as a legal entity, the frontiers of which go beyond our national financial framework.

"In the second place, we found ourselves involved in financial packages providing credit facilities to the Government of Jamaica—and here we were the only local bank in Trinidad and Tobago involved in this particular project.

"Thirdly, we were the Lead Manager in the Trinidad and Tobago/Barbados government joint-venture agreement concerning the establishment of the Arawak Cement Company."

CARICOM Travelers' Cheques

The Treaty of Chaguaramas established the Caribbean Community and Common Market (CARICOM). It was signed on July 4, 1973 in Chaguaramas, Trinidad and Tobago by Barbados, Guyana, Jamaica and Trinidad and Tobago.

One of the intentions of the Treaty was the facilitation of growth of trade and monetary and banking co-operation between the Caribbean Member Countries. In 1977 the CARICOM Multilateral Clearing System was established to settle payments between member countries.

A further result was the establishment in1980 of a Caricom Travelers' Cheque Facility denominated in Trinidad and Tobago dollars. The cheques were denominated in Trinidad and Tobago currency rather than in the currency of United States of America, as another strategy to deal with scarce United States dollars in the Caribbean. These cheques were to be used by persons who were travelling between Caricom member countries. The National Commercial Bank of Trinidad and Tobago Limited was designated the issuing authority for Caricon Travelers' Cheques.

National Commercial Bank saw this responsibility to be Issuer of the cheques, as further facilitating the strengthening of the integration of the Caricom Member Countries, as well as contributing towards a solution of the foreign currency dependency of Caricom Countries.

The project was not as successful as anticipated for many reasons. Some of these reasons were:

- Legislation had to be passed in the participating Caribbean Countries, and this happened slowly; also, in some Countries the legislation to facilitate the use of the Caricom Travellers' Cheques was never introduced in Parliament.

- Problems of currency stability within some currencies.
- Differences of discounting the cheques between different traders.
- Traditional insular attitudes between the various member Countries.

The project was eventually disbanded in December 1993. National Commercial Bank was merged into First Citizens Bank in September 1993.

Daycare Centre for Children of NCB'S Staff

Unfortunately, another prospective innovation—a children's modern Daycare/Homework Center facility owned and operated by the bank for children of bank staff—did not materialize.

The motivation was to ease the minds of parents who were concerned about their children being unsupervised between the end of school and collection of the children after normal working hours. This proposed Center did not materialize, as it was another idea whose time had not yet come.

Tobago NCB Branch in Roxborough

Roxborough Branch in Tobago was opened in December 1981 and it was closed some five years thereafter. The circumstances that led to its closure included the economic downturn in Trinidad and Tobago in the mid-1980s, and the advance in technology that facilitated servicing customers and potential customers of the branch, notwithstanding its closure.

NCB accepted the reality of the situation. Nonetheless, closure of the outlet meant that there was no physical branch structure, of any commercial bank, outside of Scarborough to serve the people of Tobago. This could be considered somewhat of a loss to the people of Tobago.

CHAPTER 7

EXPLORING THE TEMPLATE OF THE NATIONAL COMMERCIAL BANK

The Business Growth Template

Firms will be at different stages of development. Some will be in business already, some may be in expansion mode, and others may be in the conceptual stage. Thus, appropriate adaptations have to be made to cater for the emergence of particular parameters affecting different situations. Also, different economic conditions and different stages in the business environment are required to be assessed.

In addition, the sequencing of these 19 elements of The Business Growth Template will be determined by individual preferences, technological awareness and other relevant circumstances. For example, at NCB'S launch there was no recorded operational system, as all the operational manuals of the predecessor bank being their proprietary systems were not left at the bank.

Therefore, it was of significant priority that operating manuals be developed quickly and this was pioneered by Mr. Andrew Mc Eachrane, as one of his first assignments on joining the bank. The successful implementation of the operational manuals of the bank was a key factor in NCB'S success.

The economic state of the Country, and the amount, nature, and quality of the available human resources have to be taken into account. Moreover, the entrepreneur has to apply creativity, good judgment, and emotional intelligence to craft the required unique template for the business.

A Template is merely the fashioning of a system that was successfully introduced previously. Modifications and adjustments have to be made to take into account different situations, different industries, different resources and different stages of growth in the development of the business.

In the following explanation of the 19 elements of the template, their basic meaning and direction will be given but these elements will not be fully explained and developed. Each element is complex and far reaching. In fact, there are at least 50 books published and available for each element. Thus, to use and master this Prospective Template, persons intending to use it should invest adequate time and effort in researching the books appropriate to their knowledge and circumstances.

Based on the experience of the journey of the National Commercial Bank of Trinidad and Tobago, a prospective Business Growth Template for establishing and developing a business in a matured competitive industry can be formulated by adroitly following the nineteen elements of the template.

21st Century Imperative

National Commercial Bank was established in the 20th Century. Significant changes have been made in the banking industry since then. For example, previously customer convenience in banking required that there was a proper spread of a network of branches to which the customer must have easy access.

New technology reduced the necessity to have brick and mortar branches as previously. For example, at one time NCB had twenty-three branches but with the advent of new technology the network was reduced to eighteen branches without sacrificing customer convenience.

There were four main elements that changed the manner in which customers could conduct their business with the bank:

(i) Automated Business Machines (ABMs) permitted customers to conduct cash transactions during twenty-four hours a day for seven days in a week. Moreover, with the LINX interconnectivity between the competing banks, a customer could use his/her Linx Card at any ABM of any bank.

(ii) With the system of on-line banking, a customer could effect transfers between accounts from a computer at home or elsewhere.

(iii) Payments of bills could be made from smart cell phones.

(iv) APPS.— Developed by the bank and other providers established a digital platform with the potential to revolutionize personal bank credit and other operational banking systems. One example is Peer to Peer (P2P) Banking; this is a creative banking platform that makes person to person banking conveniently effected on your smart phone or tablet.

The Business Growth Template

Nineteen elements of this prospective Business Growth Template are:

(1) **Establishment of a mission, and a strategic direction and plan.** A mission expresses the company's reason for existence. The company comes into existence to provide goods or services that have an effective demand by potential customers. It is a present intention, as opposed to a vision that tends to be more futuristic. The mission points in a particular direction, and there must be an associated plan to deliver the intention. At the start of a new business it is usually premature to develop a three-year Strategic Plan.

(2) **The need for branding the business.** Branding is a means of identifying your business. It is the way customers and potential customers recognize and experience your business. A strong brand extends beyond a logo. It is reflected throughout the operations of the company, including customer service style, staff uniforms, business cards, premises, marketing materials and advertising.

(3) **Assessing the nature, strengths, and weaknesses of the main competitors.** Having an in-depth knowledge of the elements of your competitors is critical to challenge their market share. You need to know where they can be successfully challenged in their strongholds, and in what areas you have a comparative advantage, or the least comparative cost disadvantage.

(4) **Selecting customer delight as a very high priority.** Without customers there is no business. Delighting customers by virtue of price, quality, service, and consistency must therefore be given a high priority.

(5) **Identifying and providing products and services for which there is an effective demand, but the prevailing market does not provide them.** This is perhaps the greatest opportunity to impact the market. If there is a vacuum in the market place, and you move in early to fill it, you pre-empt saturation of that particular niche.

(6) **Implementation of systems to deliver operational efficiency, including the internal audit function**.

Systems are the keys to productivity. When

a system is laid out to deliver an activity, this provides the possibility of a consistent delivery for the particular operation. It is not left to the discretion of the employee.

The internal audit function represents the financial conscience of the Chief Executive. The business of the firm is so extensive that if the policies, practices and rules are not being followed, the Chief Executive cannot know, in real time, when those breaches are occurring.

It is intended that the internal audit system would capture the deviations. There is thus a strong case for the Head of Internal Audit to report directly to the Chief Executive.

(7) **Competitive terms and conditions of employment.** Without customers there is no business. Equally, without workers to serve the customers there is no business. To obtain the best possible employees, competitive terms and conditions of employment must be offered. Moreover, after engagement the employees must be shown mutual respect and caring by the management.

(8) **Engender cohesiveness in the Board of Directors.** At law, the Board controls the governance of the company. Its cohesiveness

is crucial for the success of the business. The selection of Board Members has to be carefully made for similarity of values, although different skills, experience, and professions.

(9) **Develop a strong executive management team.** The success of a business is dependent on the strength of its executive management team. Special attention has to be given to the strategies that will make the team more cohesive.

(10) **A Communication Framework for stakeholders**. Communication is the glue that keeps the business together. All activities of the business from its conception to delivery of its products and services are required to be communicated in one form or another. A communication framework for all stakeholders is thus required to optimize the operations of the business.

(11) **Cultivating an atmosphere of mutual respect between management and other staff.** Respect means different things to different people. This suggests that a corporation should establish a basic corporate standard of respect that can be added to and

modified, to accommodate changes through experience and increased knowledge.

The corporate standard of respect should include in its definition the elements of politeness, listening, keeping your word, and acting or speaking that indicate that you care about the person with whom you are interacting. Respect is also shown when you empathize with another's discomfort or family disaster.

When a culture of mutual respect is developed between employer/employee, it activates acceptance of leadership, and the empowerment of employees to contribute and innovate more deeply.

(12) **Keeping abreast of technological advances in the industry.** To ensure maintaining competitive advantage, the business must be in step with the latest technological advances, especially with respect to operations and customer service.

(13) **Establish clear corporate values.** The core values are the guiding principles that should be used by employees in discharging their respective duties. Corporate core values help employees to know what the business is

expecting from them as an Ambassador of the business. Some examples of corporate core values are: loyalty, excellence, integrity, respect, discipline, service, honesty, and commitment.

(14) **Ensure that the business is seen as a responsible Corporate Citizen.** Public perception of a business affects positively or negatively the success of that business. A business must so conduct itself that the community in which it operates believes that the Social Corporate Responsibilities **(SCR)** of the business are being properly honored.

(15) **Generate sufficient residual income to sustain and grow the business.** Without the generation of net income, the business will fail. This residual income is required to maintain employment levels, replenish stock, re-invest in the business, give a return to investors, and grow its business horizontally and vertically.

(16) **Craft a vigorous human resource policy, including training and discipline.** Continuous training of the staff is necessary. New techniques are being developed, and upgrading of skills is required for career advancement.

(17) **Implement a Productivity Outreach.** Productivity is a function of the combined efforts of management, employees, and technology. However, the basic guideline is that for the same inputs there should be greater outputs, or that at the same outputs less inputs are required.

(18) **Defining the accountabilities for and responsibilities of the critical elements of the business.** Defining the responsibilities and accountabilities of the major elements of a business are crucial for success.

Generally, the major parts of a business are: finance, marketing and sales, human resource, production, information technology and general administration. It is important that the responsibilities and accountabilities are clearly defined so that the various persons will be certain of their responsibilities.

This is important for accountability, as there should be consequences for non-performance or under performance.

(19) **Opportunities for career development.**

It is natural for a human being to want to advance or do better in life. If there is no possibility for advancement in the present work place, the employee will seek an opportunity elsewhere.

In such an event, the institutional experience, training and investment in that employee will be lost. This is one of the reasons for establishing career pathways for employees within the organization.

Assessment by an individual business

Firms will be at different stages of development. Thus, appropriate adaptations have to be made to the Business Growth Template. Also, the priority of these nineteen elements of the Template will differ depending on individual preferences.

This Business Growth Template is not a magical answer for business success. The goal is to offer some of the techniques and focus points that served NCB in its struggle to emerge. Hopefully, business entities will be able to use their unique creativity and deepened knowledge and wisdom to be more successful than would otherwise be the case.

Individual firm's assessment

To get an overview of how your business is positioned in relation to the prospective Business

Growth Template, undertake an assessment of where the business stands. The nineteen elements having being prioritized and sequenced according to your assessment, rate each element between one and ten. Mastery of the element will be scored ten, and poor or weak performance score one, with other appropriate scores between one and ten. Where there is any assessment at six or less means that the particular element has to be enhanced.

After your analysis it will be clear that there is a considerable amount of work to be undertaken. However, it can be done. It's possible! You have a better sense of direction to aim for excellence, and you have the possibility of tweaking your policies, practices and procedures to achieve your vision and mission. Remember that profits or net income is a residual figure and represents the financial outcome arising from the results of the policies, practices and procedures of the business.

Thus, if you want to improve your financial results, you have to change some of your policies, practices and procedures. Remember the familiar comment that if you keep doing the same thing, you will most likely get the same results that you want changed.

Reality of differing perspectives

For any business to formulate the precise framework to establish its Business Growth Template is a tremendous challenge. There is no one set of the nineteen elements, nor one generic set of priorities that will fit all organizations.

The matter is further complicated when there is an Executive Management Team that has to be so conditioned that its members have the perception that their views have been heard and understood, although all their points are not included in the final decision. This is necessary as the human resources experts maintain that, "what the executive creates, the executive supports."

Another angle of difficulty is shown at King Solomon's Proverbs Chapter 21:2. "Every way of a man is right in his own eyes." Expressed another way, "every man believes that his way is the right way." This adage is even more operative, the greater the intellect of the person.

The author had personal experience of this when he was an Executive Member of the five-member Executive Team, Chaired by the Governor of the Central Bank. The Team met every workday to monitor and review the operations of the financial, monetary, banking, and economic sectors of the economy, and where appropriate, take action to keep the economy of Trinidad and Tobago on an even keel. The author did not always agree with the Governor, but usually gave him the benefit of the doubt due to the Governor's superior economic knowledge and experience.

The author had functioned as an Economist in the Ministry of Finance for three years, and he believed that in certain areas he had a better grasp of the culture and economic aspirations of the people of Trinidad and Tobago, as opposed to other members of the team who did not have such exposure. However, Dr. Alexander McLeod, then Governor of the Central Bank, had extensive training and experience in economic, monetary, banking and fiscal matters and the author learned a great deal form Dr. McLeod. Of course, the author, despite his initial disagreement in some matters, had no choice but to be disciplined and support whatever was the final decision of the executive Team of the Central Bank.

Leading and managing diversity of consciousness in an Executive Team is a real challenge. The Leader has to be prepared to accept that his team will not agree with him on every occasion, but the Leader must be always fully present, compassionate and humble. Also, the team members must be magnanimous, and give their unstinted support when they do not fully agree with the leader's decisions.

CHAPTER 8

CONSOLIDATION OF THREE BANKS

Transition from National Commercial Bank to First Citizens Bank

What was the motivation for the integration of three local commercial banks? There were 4 major reasons in support of bank consolidation as follows:

(a) There was a two tier structure of fixed deposit rates, with the local banks paying on average 2% higher on fixed deposit rates than the international banks paid. This occurred because there was fierce competition between the local banks for the special customers who wished to do business with the indigenous banks.

Elimination of this disparity of 2% higher interest rates on fixed deposits would reduce, by its elimination, the expenses of the three consolidated banks and increase consolidated profits by over $30 million.

(b) There was duplication of infra structure resources such as branches, ABMs and in-branch technology.

(c) Fierce competitiveness existed between the local banks for the limited trained human resources available, and willing to risk their careers in the indigenous banking sector. This led to a skewed higher salary structure between the indigenous banks.

(d) The individual banks had developed institutional experience, competence, and customer goodwill that could have been consolidated and capitalized upon.

The Process

The process of integration began in 1991 from an initiative of Philip G. Rochford, then Chairman and Managing Director of National Commercial Bank, who organized a meeting of the Chief Executives of the three indigenous banks.

Research of attempts at integrating companies internationally showed that failure of such attempts was grounded by the fear of senior executives that they would lose their status and positions. For example, there would be one Chief Executive, one Financial Controller, one Human

Resource Manager, one Manager Operations, and one Manger of Information Technology with the 2 other similar titled managers losing their positions. Similarly, not all members of the Boards of the three banks would form the new Board of the integrated bank.

To overcome this fear of loss of jobs by senior executives, the meeting was presented with a proposed structure for the new integrated bank. Firstly, Philip G. Rochford indicated that if the process of establishing the new bank was underway he would retire before the new bank was established: he had passed age fifty-five which was the employee's optional age of retirement. Also, Rochford indicated that he would not accept an appointment as Chairman or Director on the Board of the new bank. One reason for this retirement approach was to increase the possibility of integration of the senior executives of the three indigenous banks.

Senior Executives' structure of the New Bank

The corporate structure proposed by Rochford for the New Integrated Bank rested on three pillars:

- the senior executive staff would retain their income and other terms and conditions despite being placed in a different position. Those terms would be personal and specific to them, and not to successive holders of the new integrated post.

- the major responsibilities of the bank would be allocated to officers depending on their particular training and experience in the particular fields.
- the Chief Executive of National Commercial Bank, Philip G. Rochford, would retire, having passed fifty-five years, the employees' optional age for retirement.

Formalization of intention to merge

There were three different organizational streams that could be converted into one big river:

(1) Trinidad Co-operative Bank Limited—the oldest and smallest of the three banks—had encouraged the small income-earner to save, earning the sobriquet the "Penny Bank."

(2) The second bank, Workers' Bank, was born out of the Country's labor leadership encouraging worker-members to use their back pay or other lump-sum resources to invest in share ownership of the Workers'

Bank; this Bank's Board of Directors was also heavily weighted in favor of trade unionists.

(3) The third and largest bank, The National Commercial Bank, was incorporated in 1970, as a normal commercial entity with the obligation to compete with the other six foreign banks. The branches of these foreign banks had full head office support for their managerial, technical, and operational requirements. The three merging banks had to rely on their own local resources, without the advantage of an experienced, long standing International Head Office.

New awareness

By 1992, the analysis of the operations of the three indigenous banks showed that they were competing only among themselves! This led to keen competition for the relatively small market of customers willing to risk depositing funds with the new kids on the block. This went further to cause indigenous banks to have to pay on average two percent more for fixed deposits than the foreign banks!

On the personnel side, there was only a relatively small cadre of professionals who had a commitment to work for local entities. This pushed salaries up to a premium level to secure and retain the best staff. Another negative area was weak resource allocation, duplication of heavy capital expenditure by the three indigenous banks for information technology, and duplication of branches near to each other. The three Banks agreed to consider the viability of a merged venture.

The Chief Executives of the three banks agreed that the idea appeared feasible enough to take the next step. Two of the three banks, Workers' Bank and Trinidad Co-operative Bank were under the control of the Central Bank through Section 44 of the Central Bank Act, 1964 and therefore had to get the Central Bank's permission to proceed with the project. Also, the Boards of Directors of the three banks had to agree for the relevant study to be undertaken. The Central Bank and the Boards of the three banks agreed, and a Memorandum of Agreement to proceed was signed on July 27 1992.

To honor his commitment to the chief executives of the other two indigenous banks, Chairman Rochford submitted his retirement letter of August 26 1992 to the Governor of the Central Bank of Trinidad and Tobago, as he was required at law to do. The Governor replied to this notification by letter dated September 03 1992, asking the Chairman and

Managing Director to defer his retirement pending finalization of the merger, to which the Chairman and Managing Director agreed

Merger Committee's deliberations

Following the signing of the Memorandum of Understanding to consider the possibility of a merger, a committee was formed under the Chairmanship of Dr. Terrence Farrell, then Deputy Governor of the Central Bank of Trinidad and Tobago. Ms. Amoy Chan Fong, another Senior Officer of the Central Bank and senior members from the three banks.

The Merger Committee submitted its report that the merger was feasible and recommended a course of action that included NCB being the acquiring bank, and Government holding not more than 20% of the new equity. At that point NCB had over 23,000 shareholders with the Government owning 36.4% of the shareholding. The Governor of the Central Bank and the Government had a different approach than that of the Merger Committee.

The Government's position essentially meant bringing NCB under Central Bank control by law. The other 2 banks were already under Central Bank control, so this facilitated the process, as the 23,000 shareholders would be paid for their shares, and this would give Government 100% control of the merged bank.

Merger options

There were two major options on the table. One option was that of the merger committee for an arms length negotiation with 23, 000 shareholders being satisfied that their interests were being properly served. The other option was for Central Bank to bring NCB under its control and give Government initially 100% control to justify whatever re-capitalization and funding the new entity needed for its proper flotation.

It is noteworthy to point out that National Commercial Bank had more resources than the other two merging banks combined; NCB had more branches, more deposits, more professional staff, more shareholders, more assets, more profits, more customers, and more overall staff than Trinidad Cooperative Bank and Workers' Bank combined.

As in any situation, there are different options, and the Central Bank and Government opted for what they believed was in the overall best interest of the Country.

Differences in valuation of National Commercial Bank's shares

A major controversy was that the shares of the banks, and particularly NCB'S shares, were not properly valued. The Central Bank and the Government used the Report of Ernst & Young (London) in determining the valuation of NCB'S shares.

On 22nd September 1993, the Mr. Leonard Williams, Chairman and Chief Executive Officer of First Citizens Bank handed to Mr. Alfred Gopaulsingh, Deputy Managing Director and Chief Operating Officer, as well as to Mr. Lennard Prescod, Senior General Manager of First Citizens Bank, the Ernst & Young (London) Report for their comments. Both these officers who were asked for their comments were previously senior executives of NCB and had intimate knowledge of the operations of NCB. They both had the accounting qualification of Fellow of the Chartered Certified Accountant (FCCA). Additionally, the Deputy Managing Director had an economics degree, and the Senior General Manager had an M.Sc.(Econ)

(London) degree, as well as being a Fellow of the Institute of Bankers (FCIB)

They submitted a joint reply to the Chairman of

First Citizens Bank, and copied it to the Governor of the Central Bank, Minister of Finance, and Prime Minister, and in their joint reply they had serious negative concerns about various aspects of the Report.

As fate would have it, by 31st March 1993 NCB'S Chairman and Managing Director, Philip G. Rochford, had attained sixty years, and under the terms of his employment retired at this date, but his services were retained until July 31 1993. He was therefore no longer employed in the bank, was not part of the operational process of the merger, nor invited to contribute his views on the Ernst & Young (London) Report. Rochford found out about the arrangements for dealing with the 23,000 NCB'S shareholders through the media, at the same time as the general public.

What seems clear from a post-review of the issues in contention in the Ernst & Young (London) report is that there were weighty technical and involved issues that were not resolved by judicial settlement nor adjudicated upon by the International Accounting Bodies established to set and rule on International Accounting Standards and best practice.

Moreover, for fear of breach of customer confidentiality and other litigation possibilities, the Ernst & Young (London) report was not laid in Parliament, nor made public. The effect of all of this is that the 23,000 shareholders of NCB did not know, if the valuation of their shares at ten cents per one-dollar par value share was fair and equitable.

Outcome of submission of analysis of Report

The two former NCB senior financial officers who were at that time employed by the merged First Citizens Bank undertook a skilful analysis of the Ernst & Young (London) Report; the analysis showed possible flaws in some of the reasoning and assumptions in the Report.

However, in submitting their report to the Chairman and Chief Executive Officer of First Citizens Bank, they made the error of copying their joint report to the Prime Minister, as well as to the Minister of Finance and the Central Bank. First Citizens Bank immediately terminated their services for essentially breach of confidentiality of the bank's business.

These two officers did err on technical grounds, but equally it can be said, that in all the circumstances they were technically correct, as both Ministers had a right to be made aware of the situation. For example, the Minister of Finance had used information from the Ernst & Young (London) Report to transfer the assets and liabilities of NCB to First Citizens Bank Limited by a Vesting Order over the weekend of Saturday September 11 1993 and Sunday September 12 1993.

In the case of the Prime Minister, as Head of the Government of Trinidad and Tobago, he ought to have been advised that with respect to Government connected accounts, the Report assumed certain actions by the Government that the Prime Minister ought to be aware of.

Nonetheless, it can be legitimately maintained that the two dismissed officers used the wrong process to disclose confidential business of the bank to sources external to the corporate entity. Moreover, the emotional impact of the nature of the information included in the Report clouded the fact that they were not the designated authority in the bank to make such disclosures to sources outside the bank.

An interesting aspect

An interesting aspect of the drama of the merger is that a draft of the Ernst & Young (London) Report, on the affairs of the business of the National Commercial Bank, was referred to these two senior accounting officers of the Bank on 22 September 1993, and they replied on 29 September 1993, but the merger was legally effected on 12 September 1993. This challenged Report was used in establishing the value of NCB'S shares, and NCB'S shareholders were already notified by a letter of offer from the Central Bank to buy their shares at ten cents per one-dollar par value share. This put the Authorities in a quandary, so the First Citizens Bank used a legitimate process to terminate the services of these two officers.

It was unfortunate that Mr. Lennard Prescod. Senior General Manager and Mr. Alfred Gopaulsingh, Deputy Managing Director and Chief Operating Officer of First Citizens Bank (formerly of National Commercial Bank) services were terminated, despite their Professional Excellent Competence.

Be that as it may, the differences of accounting opinion and treatment of accounts were never resolved, so that the 23,000 shareholders of National Commercial Bank do not know whether the value of ten cents for each share they owned was a true and fair value of their investment. It is instructive to 'Google' Ernst & Young for information on their litigation worldwide. However, "The horse has already bolted from the stable."

Implementation of the merger

The merger had been under formal discussion since July 1992, and there was public knowledge of this. However, all the elements to bring the merger into effect were not in place. For example, on 9th March 1993 First Citizens Bank Limited was registered with a nominal capital of $500,000 to acquire and take over as a going concern the business and assets of the three banks to be merged. There was an advertisement that the new bank, First Citizens Bank Limited, would be started in August 1993, and a subsequent advertisement advised that First Citizens Bank Limited would begin operations in September 1993.

The Bombshell

Unfortunately, a copy of one of the draft reports of Ernst & Young (London), a reputable international accounting firm, was leaked to the weekend BOMB Newspapers, and on its front page edition of **Friday10th September 1993** the Headline was **$1b NCB DEBT HEADACHE.**

The Governor of the Central Bank from his information and enquiries believed that there was a real possibility that there would be a run on the three banks when they opened on Monday 13ᵗʰ September 1993. Accordingly, the Governor and the Minister of Finance acted swiftly on Saturday 11ᵗʰ September 1993 and Sunday 12ᵗʰ September 1993 to put in place the legal requirements, including a vesting order to transfer the assets of the banks. These actions ensured that when the three banks opened on Monday 13ᵗʰ September 1993, the merger would be legally "a fait accompli."

The horse is out of the stable. Nothing can be usefully done at this stage. Even if action is taken now, the Central Bank is protected under the legislation, unless it can be proven that the Central Bank acted with malice aforethought. There was no evidence adduced that the Central Bank acted with malice aforethought with respect to its actions and decisions in merging the three indigenous banks.

Conflict of interests in shares' valuation

The process used by the Central Bank to value the shares of the Trinidad Co-operative Bank, Workers' Bank and National Commercial Bank was not considered to be appropriate as adjudicated by the Privy Council in its judgment in a case brought by Gulf Insurance Limited, a significant shareholder in Trinidad Cooperative Bank. This litigation brought by Gulf Insurance Limited in 1993 took10 years to be settled eventually at the Privy Council in 2003.

In part of that judgment, the Privy Council ruled that the Central Bank erred in not getting **an independent valuation,** as in all the circumstances the Ernst & Young (London) Report could not be considered an independent valuation. However, in that Gulf Insurance Limited litigation, the Privy Council believed that harm was not done to the Trinidad Cooperative Bank shareholder.

My considered view is that had an NCB shareholder gone to the Privy Council, its determination would have substantially increased the share value of the 23,000 members of the public who were shareholders of NCB. This view is based on the judicially unresolved questionable assumptions on which the valuation was based.

There should have been no actions or circumstances to suggest a conflict of interests by the merging authorities. The following facts are critical; they underscore the principle that the merger process should not only be equitable but must be perceived as such by the minority shareholders and the general public:

1.   The Central Bank is the regulatory authority for the banking system, and two of the three

merging banks were under Sec. 44 control of the Central bank Act prior to approaching the Central Bank to consider a merger

2. Prior to the merger the Minister of Finance as Corporation Sole held 36.4 percent of the shares of NCB and over 50 percent of the shares of the Workers' Bank (1989) Limited.

3. The Central Bank had control of 50 percent of the shares of the Trinidad Co-operative Bank Limited prior to the merger of September 12, 1993.

4. By vesting order the Minister of Finance, presumably on the advice of the Central Bank, transferred the assets and liabilities of the three merging banks to First Citizens Bank Limited and its associate company, Taurus Limited. First Citizens Bank Limited (FCB) originally had the Government of Trinidad and Tobago as its principal shareholder.

5. NCB was placed under Sec. 44 control of the Central Bank Act simultaneously with the establishment of the merger on September 12 1993.

6. In view of the high level of share ownership or control by the Minister of Finance and the Central Bank of the three merging banks, the

minority shareholders of the merging banks should have been given an opportunity to analyze and assess the values being placed on their shares. The same people who will benefit from vesting the assets and liabilities of the three merging banks into the First Citizens Bank Group ought to have obtained an independent valuation of the respective shares. This independent valuation was not undertaken, as determined by the Privy Council in the Gulf Insurance Limited litigation against the Central Bank, with respect to the valuation of the shares of Trinidad Co-operative Bank Limited.

Unfortunately, no shareholder of National Commercial Bank was willing and able to contest litigation against the Authorities that would undoubtedly be referred to the Privy Council. Thus, it has not been judicially determined whether the shareholders of National Commercial Bank got a fair deal with their shares of $1.00 par value being valued by the Authorities at ten cents per share. Moreover, NCB'S shareholders were not even given an option, at fair values, for a share ownership conversion, of their NCB shares for shares in the new Bank,

First Citizens Bank Limited. The 23,000 minority shareholders of National Commercial Bank had no opportunity to negotiate with the Authorities for the price of the sale of their shares.

Even at the questionable value of 10 cents per share, NCB'S 23,000 minority shareholders, in equity, should have been given an option for cash **or** one (1) First Citizens Bank share for every ten (10) NCB shares held.

CHAPTER 9

THE NEW BANK—FIRST CITIZENS BANK

The history of First Citizens Bank proved that the merger concept was valid, effective and profitable. The primary losers were the 23,000 shareholders who birthed the National Commercial Bank as a public company. If they were given the option of either a conversion of a certain number of NCB shares for a share in the new bank, or the cash value of an NCB share, this would have been equitable. For example, using the Central Bank's valuation, ten NCB shares equal one First Citizen Bank share.

This would have been justified on at least three grounds: (a) there was some doubt about the low value placed on NCB shares and this would ensure the shareholder got a just reward for the faith in investing in NCB. For example, the balance of house mortgage loans that were six months in arrears were completely written off from the equity share capital of NCB on the assumption that the real estate value of house and land was zero. (b) some loans that were classified as bad loans in the Report on NCB were repaid by the date on which the Report was referred to the two senior officers of the Bank for their review and comments. (c) loans of State Agencies whose interest were six months in arrears were completely written off the equity share capital of NCB, on the assumption that the Government would not honor their guarantees and other obligations that were undertaken. The above three grounds and other suspect factors led to a value of ten cents being placed on an NCB share.

Post-merger

Following the merger there were four major stages of operations. The first stage was the reconciliation of the differences in culture, systems and vision of the three banks. This led to internal rivalry among staff and did not facilitate initial smooth operations.

The second stage was the appointment of a foreign Chief Executive, Mr. Len Busse from United States of America. The view was that such a person would have no "sacred cows" arising from any of the three banks, and he would use his professionalism to launch the bank successfully. In addition, Mr. Busse was given a mandate to sell the merged bank to a foreign bank with him being given a commission on its sale. This second stage was not as successful as anticipated and Mr. Busse's appointment was ended.

The third stage started with the appointment of Mr. Larry Howai as the Chief Executive. This was a strategic move for four reasons (a) the selection was made through public competitive applications for the post (b} Mr. Howai had worked in senior positions at NCB and Workers' Bank, in addition to Development Finance Company. Moreover when he worked at NCB, he was given a scholarship by NCB to complete his professional training in Accountancy in Canada. (c) Mr. Howai had proven his worth in the performance of duties he had been previously assigned to perform in the merged bank (d) he had demonstrated his competence and efficiency in his various appointments at NCB, Development Finance Company, Workers' Bank, and at the initial merged bank.

The fourth stage, under Mr. Howai, was the streamlining of First Citizens Bank, its integration and reconstruction, culminating in First Citizens Bank winning many international awards for being a progressive commercial bank.

The crowning glory of success for First Citizens Bank Limited was a successful issue of shares to the public in July 2013. This First Citizens Bank's Initial Public Offering of shares was issued at $22.00 per share; 48,495,665 shares valued $1.1 billion, representing 19.3% of the equity, leaving the Government as the majority shareholder of First Citizens Bank Limited.

Political interference

It is interesting to note that First Citizens Bank was successful despite the attempts at political interference in its operations. Two such attempts were made public. In July 1997 Mr. Guy Hannays resigned as Chairman of First Citizens Bank, and in September 2004 Mr. Kenneth Gordon resigned as Chairman of First Citizens Bank. Both Chairmen indicated that they did not agree with the manner of political interference in the governance of the operations of First Citizens Bank.

CHAPTER 10

REVOLUTION IN THE BANKING SYSTEM OF TRINIDAD AND TOBAGO

What did this revolution in the local commercial banking system have on the progress of Trinidad and Tobago? The effects were mainly qualitative but significant, as it engendered, through the demonstration effect, the international banks to use their tremendous resources in new directions.

The principal impacts that National Commercial Banking provided were:

(a) Transformation of the total banking system to be more sensitive, than hitherto, to the local needs of the people of the Country.

(b) Focus more particularly on the small income customer through better deposit rates, and integrity loans.

(c) Opening up the market for home mortgages and land loans for house construction

(d) Local incorporation of the majority of international banks, rather than being merely branches of foreign banks registered to do business in Trinidad and Tobago.

(e) Expansion of the local Stock Exchange Market, with new opportunities for individuals to own part of the patrimony of Trinidad and Tobago.

(f) Opened up opportunities of employment, not previously available, without discrimination,.

(g) Provided through training and experience development of local professional and managerial staff to extend to the wider banking community, and the community in general.

(h) Increased use of local professionals, as service providers to the banking industry.

(i) Support of Government's strategic creative plan for the diversification and transformation of the economy through a creative capital financing structure for Point Lisas Development Corporation. This bridging financing facilitated empowering the economic diversification process, as it enabled the PLIPDECO Estate to initiate the construction of facilities for prospective tenants of the Estate.

(j) Reduction of gender bias of females in the work place, as well as providing special products for females in the banking system.

(k) Widened the concept of what is the Corporate Social Responsibility (CSR) of an exemplary Corporate Citizen.

(l) Provided financial counseling and business support services for small and medium sized businesses. This included being more sensitive to foreclosing on mortgage housing loans, especially where there was clearly commitment and appropriate action to repay the debt.

(m) Lifted the self-confidence and self-esteem of the Citizens of Trinidad and Tobago by demonstrating that Citizens of Trinidad and Tobago could manage financial institutions.

(n) Provided mortgage loans for housing and land loans for house construction on 90% financing terms, not previously available.

(o) Published profits for the first 22 years of NCB'S existence. Accounts for its 23rd year, just prior to its merger into First Citizens Bank, are in contention.

(p) Provided a nationwide network of branches, cutting edge technology, properly trained and experienced staff, goodwill of over 200,000 customers, a significant deposit base, and capital reserves arising from the increased value of NCB owned branch network real estate: these elements facilitated the success of the three indigenous banks being merged into First Citizens Bank Limited.

(q) Increased the total deposits from $4.5 million in the first year in1970 to over $1.5 billion in its final year in 1993.

CHAPTER 11

MORAL OF THE BANKING STORY

Your life's joyous expansion

What is the purpose of one's journey on entering this world? Observation reveals that you learn, grow and in the process look for joy, happiness, or fulfillment. However, over time you need to develop clarity on what you want your life to be dedicated to.

It is clear that there will be always blockages, distractions, hurdles and difficulties: that is called LIFE. The only person who has no problems in this life is the person who is dead.

What is the contribution you wish to make by the time of your death? You have your dreams. Live them! The author lived his dreams joyously, although his father died when he was two years old. He had a brother and sister two and three years older respectively, but he did not have the luxury of a father figure when growing up. His mother had her own struggles, and the trauma of the Second

World War (1939-1945) with its economic effects made matters worse.

The author's tipping point occurred when at 24 years of age, he witnessed his then Supervisor, who was old enough to be his father, being publicly abused and humiliated in the worst possible manner by the boss of his Supervisor. Thereupon, the author resolved that he would not expose himself to the possibility of such an event. He re-dedicated himself to work towards becoming personally skilled and employment independent.

The author's breakthrough came by reading, thinking, and multi-skilled training while being ferociously aware and present. The point is that he followed his dreams. You can also successfully follow your dreams. The author decided what he wanted and he did not give up on the struggle. Courage requires you to keep moving towards your high hopes, although the successful outcome is not certain. Courage demands that despite setbacks to what you want to achieve, you will relentlessly press on, although the passion has faded for the activities you initially contemplated. Be courageous with respect to your dreams.

You can excel and leave your unique legacy of which you can be proud. There is greatness within you. You are engineered for success and designed for accomplishment. Be successful! Put your attention on your intentions and you will soar like an eagle.

Be clear on what you want. Take persistent, relevant, and massive action on your mission and you will excel. You can do it. Manifest your potential and greatness. It's possible. You can be the best expression of yourself.

The Commercial Banking Dream

What was the dream of the Country in 1970 for National Commercial Banking? After all was said and done, what was the "value vision" of The National Commercial Bank?

Simply put, NCB initially focused on helping individuals and firms to enlarge their banking relationships to obtain better financial value for them. This was accomplished through a framework that rested on confidentiality of customers' business, competence of the employees of NCB, and overall increasing the net financial value of customers. Moreover, this was done in a public display of distinction compared to the international commercial banks operating in Trinidad and Tobago.

What NCB achieved did not depend on "rocket science." Every individual has the potential of greatness within himself or herself. You can be the best expression of yourself: clarify what you want, have confidence in yourself, and take massive relevant action in keeping with your mission. Have the courage to honor the struggle of life, and pursue your dreams relentlessly.

This model of action is intended to minimize the difficulties and maximize the upside or great opportunities available. Of course, this should reflect the meaning that you give to the lifestyle that you want to enjoy, and the legacy that you want to create—ultimately creating your value.

Power of One

You are only one person, but you have the power to change any situation that you confront with clarity, determination, massive relevant action and belief in your Divine heritage. You can be an instrument of positive change for the benefit of your Society. However, simply remember that to achieve anything of great significance, you must nurture and mobilize a group of like-minded persons. Anything of significance worth achieving requires that you have a support group to keep your momentum.

Generate your support community to guarantee your success. Above all, let your aspirations extend beyond yourself. Having a dream merely for yourself alone does not do justice to the impact you can have on the forward march of humanity.

Make everyday the best that you are capable of delivering. If you do this on a consistent basis, you will be on your way to be a Masterpiece in your flow of life.

Finally, it was a profound privilege and a daunting responsibility to participate in the journey to shift the needle of commercial banking life in Trinidad and Tobago positively, and to take a step in raising consciousness of Society.

EPILOGUE BY MR. NAZEER SULTAN, FORMER SENIOR MANAGER AT NATIONAL COMMERCIAL BANK AND FIRST CITIZENS BANK

It was the author's good fortune to have someone contribute the Epilogue who worked as a Senior Manager for fifteen years at the National Commercial Bank, and twelve years at First Citizens Bank. His perspective, being involved at both banks, will enrich the overall assessment of the journey of National Commercial Banking in Trinidad and Tobago.

EPILOGUE
Commentary on National Commercial Banking in Trinidad and Tobago

Nazeer Sultan

A. A FEW OBSERVATIONS

Let me begin by thanking the author for his courage in inviting feedback from individuals who caused him some "disappointment by their lack of passionate observance" (to use his construct). Probably he hoped that with the passage of years, memory would desert or grow hazy, more generous interpretations and appreciation may descend, or benign kindness prevail. I cannot promise any of the above and remain convinced that deep down, Phillip Guy Rochford would want none of that. I think I know the man.

Before responding to my boss's specific request, let me contextualize my contribution with a few opening observations:

Observation #1. Writing this book some 23 years after leaving the Bank, carries advantages and disadvantages. On the positive side:

a) It provides a space for mindful reflection, making it a bit easier to temper emotions, prejudices and preferences. A more balanced and objective view is likely to manifest.

b) Hindsight beats foresight in accounting for organizational performance and formulating causal stories. We can also amass the evidence to support our positions.

c) A longer-term perspective affords the luxury to witness the true impact of our work - the good, the bad and even the ugly.

On the negative side:

a) Despite our best efforts, memory may falter in bringing full accuracy and completeness to our conclusions. We may unintentionally miss critical pieces.

b) We may lose sight of nuanced interpretations about realities and challenges of the times, resulting in sub-optimal conclusions.

c) We may not have access to the necessary documentation to support our positions.

Observation #2. This relates to challenges facing the participant observer. The author led the Bank from its inception until his departure. This is both blessing and curse. On the positive side:

a) He had privileged information which he admitted that in some cases, he deliberately did not share as a matter of leadership choice. This information, now revealed, may show more clearly the 'inner workings' of the bank.

b) As leader, he knew the intended plays and plots, putting him in the best position to link many of the pieces - the intended strategy.

c) He can provide us with a deeper understanding of his work as NCB Chief.

On the negative side:

a) His closeness to intention can blur his vision and a full acceptance and recognition of the manifest, may prove difficult.

b) How do we judge our own behavior and performance? The possible loss of objectivity and inclination to convenient meaning-making, can be challenging to the best of us.

Let me hasten to add that I too, suffer from the afflictions mentioned earlier and face similar challenges, albeit of a lesser order. For purposes of transparency, I must convey that I worked at the National Commercial Bank from 1978 to the merger, and thereafter, for 12 years at First Citizens Bank - a grand total of 27 years. I had the privilege of seeing first hand, the transition to, and early transformational work of First Citizens Bank. I served in senior leadership positions in both entities, leading the functional areas of Training, Manpower Planning and Development, Corporate Planning, Consumer Lending, Regional Branch banking at NCB and Corporate Planning, Marketing and Advertising, Regional branch banking and HR at First Citizens Bank. Building capabilities based on embracing the best of the past, disrupting the status quo appropriately and allowing evidence-based practices to hold sway, was the mantra I sought to observe. I honored it faithfully - or so I hope.

In essence, mine was the opportunity to lead the crafting and design of what can be referred to as the 'social capital'. It was a privilege to continue the NCB story and to exorcise aspects of its operations and blend it with the best of the other partners – Trinidad Co-operative Bank and Workers' Bank - as we took the National Banking project to another level.

What we need to unambiguously acknowledge, is the huge presence of NCB at the inception of the merger. This cannot be denied. There are some of us who felt that there was a definite intention to downplay this, replacing it with a less generous interpretation - the rise and fall of NCB. This may well be true, but I'd rather concentrate on thanking PG for this book, because if my memory serves me right, the only other book dealing directly and with some detail on NCB, was written some years ago entitled 'On Becoming First'. I have read it many times, in part motivated by the feeling that it was incomplete, in spite of claims of truthfulness and illumination by reviewers R Balgobin and M King. Without evidence generated by human asset impact analysis on competitive advantage and growth acceleration, claims such as which organization was paternalistic and which was aggressive, remain speculative and self-serving at best, just as the 'Profile in history' chapter of the said book.

Still, we must embrace some of these alternative facts about what NCB and the others brought to the party if we are to truly understand the challenges faced by First Citizens Bank at inception and the social capital drivers that were deployed to complement its financial and related strategies. However, in this new work by PG, I've found a piece of the missing. Thank you PG for the additions and placing NCB in proper context... a positive step in consciousness building.

Having made these initial observations, I will now address the following:

DID THE BOOK DELIVER ON ITS INTENTIONS?
NCB STRATEGIES, POLICIES, PROGRAMS AND PEOPLE - AND THE IMPACT
CRITICAL OMISSIONS
CHALLENGES IN APPLYING THE LESSONS TODAY
CONCLUSION

B. DID THE BOOK DELIVER ON ITS INTENTIONS?

By his own book-writing standards, PG was not very ambitious on this occasion. A big task he was committed to; but in his words, he simply wanted to tell the true story of NCB and to provide an initial set of policies that can deepen management strategies today.

Why this focus? Is there an information/knowledge gap? Are there contradictions and untruths about NCB? Is his work as leader of NCB not understood or appreciated? Are our enterprises still failing and uncompetitive? Are we still strangers to the art of creating and reinventing practices that serve institutions? Is the work of national development still largely undone? Or is it a deeper awakening of just how difficult it is to effect change and the over-estimation of the power of office and chief, in such endeavor?

These lessons are gladly welcomed because there is a dearth of detailed management lessons applicable to Trinidad and Tobago. The CLICO inquiry provided some interesting lessons in corporate governance, but the remit was different in scope. A few years ago, Dr. Terrence Farrell, in a presentation to the Transparency Institute, spoke of the "broken institutions all around us... limping, pretending to function."[1] His focus however was not on business entities, but on public institutions. More recently, J. Khandan, in a paper entitled 'Are oil and gas smothering the private sector in Trinidad and Tobago'[2] argues that unfortunately, there are no empirical studies on the country's private sector that can provide relevant guidance. He concludes from his research that most Trinidad and Tobago firms in the non-petroleum sector are either stagnant or declining.

In this context, PG's latest book is a welcome addition to the literature. He not only documents in some detail, his mission, strategies, plans, obstacles and achievements, but also offers us management advice (from lessons learnt) through his 19 Elements Template. Throughout, he remains in my estimate, simple, factual, objective, fair and reasonable. He must be commended for his coverage - wide and deep - with a deliberate, mature, emotional distance-keeping. This is really difficult to do by office holders in these parts, more so as It puts the final piece in his own performance assessment. I give him a pass in this area.

C. <u>NCB STRATEGIES, POLICIES, PROGRAMS AND PEOPLE - AND THE IMPACT</u>

PG covered all the management bases. A review of the management literature over the last century, would confirm this. He covered the territory from many vantage points:

Vision (reconstruction of the economy, small man place in the sun)

Outcome (revolution in the banking system of T&T)

Strategic (mission, strategies, policies)

Operational (accounting, branches, credit, HR)

Values (Bank's basis, Purpose, Creed, Principles)

Action (network, products, services)

Long term (strategic direction, plans and pillars)

Short term (tactical interventions)

Urgent (the bombshell, audited financial statements, business failures)

Important (communication framework, train staff, sufficient residual income)

Traditional (business growth, staff management)

Breakthrough (responsible corporate citizen, women in management)

Routine (full range of services)

Creative (Toastmasters, Steel pan project, Play of the month)

The hard (profitability, technology)

The soft (Brand, culture, critical thinking)

Products (Chaconia, Land loans, Home Ownership, Life insured savings)

People (scholarships, training centre, Banking Institute)

Board (expert knowledge, banking experience)

Executive (potential to limit growth, lack of passionate observers)

Staff (loyalty, service oriented, confidence and competence)

Managers (faithful to follow the tenets and principles of commercial banking

Customers (convenience, confidentiality, relationship-banking)

Shareholders (adequate dividends, share value)

Challenge (public confidence, finance traps)

Opportunity (neglected segments, marketing mix)

Builders (supportive elements, the national community)

Destroyers (a possible fundamental mistake, NCB is ambushed)

Nationalistic (self confidence, self esteem, development of citizens)

Regional (CARICOM initiatives)

Personal (his narrative, ambition, conditioning, unique legacy)

Organizational (structure of new bank)

Political interference (government agents on the NCB board)

Independence (board strengths in finance, labor, business, law and academia)

Controversy (racial and color discrimination, share valuation, conflict of interest)

Agreement (national political support)

Disappointment (lack of interest by members of management)

Hope (transition from NCB to FCB and Nationals Conquering Banking)

What a journey - little missing. I must confess that the classifications - both selection and assignment of Rochford elements - are my doing. This will prove useful when I address later the relevance of his lessons. Now let's focus on the impact of the above.

NCB's presence certainly transformed the landscape of banking in Trinidad and Tobago, making it more sensitive to the needs of the people and providing among other things,

- a place for the small income customer
- innovative products that fostered home and land ownership with the intention of promoting greater self responsibility
- an enduring sense of corporate social responsibility - a concept relatively unknown in that era
- use of nationalistic themes that promoted greater pride among the citizenry
- a cadre of professional, managerial and operative bankers, equipped with a 'change' mindset given the quantity and diversity of initiatives they absorbed
- profitable operations - a key business metric

When one considers the challenges, resource constraints and expectations, this is indeed an impressive record.

D. CRITICAL OMISSIONS

It is my considered view, that a significant omission in this book, is NCB's impact on the development of First Citizens Bank. Maybe this careful treading, bordering benign acknowledgement, is due to:

a)   The author's inability to access relevant data.
b)   His choice to deliberately say little... leaving it for others to recognize.
c)   A less than full recognition of the real work done by his charges that he empowered to take action.

Without doubt, NCB's impact on First Citizens Bank was huge. PG did acknowledge the NCB inputs in more branches, deposits, professional staff, assets, profits, customers and overall operative staff. But as a senior manager in the new entity, tasked with leading responsibilities in the soft areas, as well as the early Transformation charge, I saw firsthand, how these assets were used by First Citizens Bank to build the franchise. The larger talent pool, the national reach of the branch network, the credit quality and general enterprise risk management (due to the harsh lessons of the past), the nationalistic themes, the greater ethnic and gender diversity and most importantly, the change mindset deliberately cultured by becoming NCB - these were all factors that, by virtue of their quality and sheer scale, disproportionately shaped the fledgling First Citizens Bank. From my vantage point, there was much more in common between NCB and the early days of First Citizens Bank, in terms of strategic themes and DNA qualities, than shows up in PG's account.

Other omissions include:

a) the Supervisory Control System that was aimed at installing a greater productivity orientation at the branch level. This paid huge dividends in keeping labor costs at an acceptable level while ensuring union buy-in. This provided a practical framework for the exercise of supervisory responsibilities, the first rung of the leadership ladder.

b) the design and installation of Customer Care Standards for major areas of the customer interface including acknowledgement, waiting time, transaction time and branch appearance. With these operational standards, staff could now make the link between their actions and service delivery. This created greater service consciousness throughout the organization. This system was deepened in the First Citizens Bank era.

c) NCB's Management Trainee Program was a critical pillar in the bank's managerial development effort and remained one of the better developmental programs for university graduates for many years. With an emphasis on a unique leadership mindset, growth from within was a key career management philosophy and this program provided a cadre of managers who continue to serve First Citizens Bank up to today. Visit any First Citizens Bank office today and witness the effect of this initiative.

d) The involvement of Head Office professional staff, in NCB's recoveries work. While the initial intention may have been to deal with the immediate challenge of collecting on outstanding loans, it did expose some of these 'office fine minds' to the realities of banking and business acumen. This experience I drew on heavily when I made the transition from functional management to Banking in the middle of my career. This is where the rubber hits the road and was a critical pathway to Executive Leadership development.

To close off the topic of omissions, let's talk financials. The beneficial treatment given to non-performing loans in the merger arrangement, proved a significant asset to First Citizens Bank - a tiny fact with giant implications for First Citizens Bank's future viability. And finally, the unspoken. A proper valuation of the assets of NCB, following on the ruling of the Privy Council regarding Trinidad Co-operative Bank's valuation, would have uncovered the uncomfortable truth that NCB was far stronger and operationally sound, than the story told at the time of merger. Indeed, history is written by the survivors. Thanks PG for providing some long overdue clarification.

E. <u>CHALLENGES IN APPLYING THE LESSONS TODAY</u>

When we manage in routine environments, we manage predictability. In PG's time, the business environment can be described as routine although the political and developmental challenges complicated the situation a bit. But today we live in a new era. Customer behavior is fickle, digital technology is disruptive, competition comes from unlikely sources. Welcome to the age of faster, cheaper, better... with fewer resources. It's a complex landscape that's constantly moving. In all of this, the boom and bust of a Dutch-diseased economy, is ever-present in Trinidad and Tobago. So it's no surprise that today's work experience is far removed from past decades. How do we act decisively without having clear direction? What lessons can be drawn from the NCB story? What mind-set and practices can serve organizations today?

It takes a courageous man in these VUCA times, (VOLATILE, UNCERTAIN, COMPLEX, AMBIGUOUS) to distill lessons from the past - a different past with mixed reviews - and suggest their relevance to today. However, there are some of us who believe that he is in a good position to make that case. I am one of those. The difficulties of managing in a VUCA world and managing multi-generations were similar to problems facing PG in the '70s.

He has invited us to consider his 19 Elements Template and its relevance today for competing in mature markets. He allows for adaptation given the situation, and sequencing options driven by individual preferences. All the bases of managerial action are covered and with some much needed nuances. However, the squeaking wheel need not get greased all times, especially at the expense of what really matters. In other words, this total coverage approach preempts any specific focus on the things that impact the most. I think that the effectiveness of the Template can be enhanced by being aligned to 3 broad themes that are pivotal for organizational success.

Strategy Formulation & Alignment

Nationalism was the rallying call of the NCB. To his credit, PG's strategy execution shone brightest when it came to communication, marketing and advertising (all key tenets of his Template). It could have been felt. But there was also a non-alignment to the whole, an absence of numbers, that significantly compromised the intended impact and the mobilization of the entire organization. Pieces just did not fit or make sense to some of us, or maybe it was too much to absorb.

Fast-forward to today. The standard company mission speaks of "building sustainable, profitable companies", "delivering increased value to stakeholders", "engaging customer and staff experiences in a corporate responsible manner". This is a balancing act requiring strategy formulation and execution that's not just be respectful, but reverential to stakeholders.

Strategy now, more than ever before, is about harnessing insights to make choices on where to compete, how to win and how best to optimize stakeholder value. More than articulating what's to be done, it requires alignment, specifically the alignment of People, Work Processes, Structure, Management Processes and Rewards to generate a high performance culture. It is through this alignment that co-authorship, involvement and translation can be effected at all levels of the organization. And it works best when data and feedback are used to guide corrective action. We need to more robustly run the numbers. Indeed, as Demming the quality guru reminded us some years ago, "Without data, you are just another person with an opinion."

In my view, the 19 Elements Template treats too lightly with the critical areas of discerning key priorities, linking them to stakeholder value in a practical manner and creating alignment, from boardroom to ground floor.

Culture and The Experience Economy

In mature markets, one of the key brand differentiators is the Experience, and those organizations that effectively build a culture around it, are rewarded with brand loyalty and willingness of customers to pay a premium.

PG had a hint of this when, in discussing Branding, he saw it as beyond the logo (which of course, it is). "It is reflected throughout the operations and includes service, style, uniform, business cards, premises, marketing materials and advertisement". He understood some of the requirements - Values, Corporate Principles, Five Pillars etc.- but today, in these busy times with short attention spans, the job of branding is bigger than branding. If organizations wish to retain customers today, their approach must evolve past simply branding to culture-building and creating engaging experiences consistently.

This requires insightful customer research, meaningful value propositions, and a positive engagement experience for both customers and employees. The values, the appeal, the principles of branding must reflect a consistent and compelling portrayal. In every interface with the customer and interaction with staff, this delightful engagement must be present. This reality is as simple as it is complex. Customer delight is the flipside of staff engagement. Customer branding and employment branding must connect. Talent is the prime vehicle through which a delightful customer experience is delivered. All this points directly to one pivotal area that is key to brand-building - culture and the employee experience.

We must never forget that employees are value creators, value sustainers and value destroyers. While the traditional workforce valued loyalty, hierarchy and rule-based formality, the younger generation is looking for growth and development, work life integration, transparency, collaboration and inclusivity. They want to find purpose and meaning in their work. This is not the work of traditional HR. This is the job of culture-building - embedding qualities and values in the entire organization and keeping them alive in the hearts and minds of employees.

We need to know our employees with the same discernment as marketing knows customers. We need to combine the traditional functionalities with dynamic social interaction. The embrace of social media with its attendant benefits and challenges, can prove useful here in meeting these aspirations crafting delightful experiences using research, data and feedback in an ongoing manner. This is the age of voice, and not of the broadcasting order.

Consider this. Centuries ago, bankers in Florence created cultures known as the Medici effect by encouraging diversity of thinking, embracing artists, architects, philosophers and bankers - transporting and aligning ideas from different domains. Getting the generations to work together, learning from each other, is easier said than done. But this is where opportunity lies, and it takes courage. PG possessed it.

Driven by his insight for talent back in the 70s, he assembled a relatively young, diverse and ambitious team of graduates. The space was provided intentionally or otherwise and most of the drivers of engagement - Voice, Autonomy, Mastery, and Purpose - were given some space. A bold move by a brave man, but not without flaws. As it turned out, the journey, especially with young ambitious minds, needed to have allowed for the collision of thinking without compromising unity of purpose. Probably 'the lack of interest' by members of the executive team on certain issues can now be more fully understood. How do we deal with resistance today? The options of today are not as simple as choosing A over B, or "checkmate" as posited by the author. The wisdom of the group must be intentionally sought, or else the creative capability of the organization may suffer. This is a valuable lesson for those seeking to build their brand and culture around an Experience.

In my view, the 19 Elements Template needed to be more targeted and intentional about culture building and the 'experience' opportunity. It is a huge opportunity for organizational success today and the task of building shared understanding around it, is key. But tapping into it is not for the faint-hearted. It requires leadership to see the culture work needed for customers and employees, and it takes courage to do something about it. No strategy, no matter how ingenious, has any chance of succeeding, "if it is born in the minds of a few and carried in the hearts of none". (Henry Kissinger).

Leadership

The 19 Elements Template doesn't specifically address leadership although it can be inferred from the author's references to having a strong executive team and mutual respect between employees and management. But management and leadership are not the same thing. Leadership is so integral to organizational success, that I feel compelled to bring it centre-stage and there is no better subject matter for this discussion, than the man himself, PG Rochford.

McKinsey defines good leadership as a critical part of organizational health. Effective leadership is about setting the right priorities, building and aligning processes, mobilizing hearts and minds, and delivering results. From his account, was PG up to the task? Before we put this to rest, it is important to remember that the challenge posed to this leader was a difficult balancing act. He wanted to transform the banking industry, making it more sensitive to local needs, address the employment bias, get locals involved in the commanding heights of the economy, build national pride and talent and also generate a profit - "residual income that is not obscene" (PG's term). This he achieved. Period. No spinning of story or selective use of alternative facts, can alter or diminish this record.

To follow a leader, we look for work ethic, composure, passion for work, optimism, values and beliefs and tolerance for diversity. We also look up to someone who's bold yet gracious, considerate, intellectual and warm. I had the privilege of witnessing most of these qualities from this man. He was a man on a mission. "Whatever life deals me, I will handle with God's help" was his credo.

The tipping point, seeing his boss publicly abused, influenced his career deeply. He vowed to be independent, but also recognized that we must learn and grow or become obsolete. He held himself to the same high standards he expected of others. The times in the country, the political challenges, the aspirations of its people demanded a certain type of leadership, one generally labeled "heroic leadership" - a dominant leader driving for results, almost single-handedly. That was PG. That was then. Is the hero leader right for now?

Business models and leadership requirements have been transformed. However, there is little practical discussion on how to re-tool leaders to meet the VUCA requirements. There is no doubt that we need to be more deliberate in our leadership development effort to meet the demands of greater inclusion, disruption, collaboration, diversity and purpose and meaning - the new work realities. We must watch how we lead. It's not merely about getting people to, but also an invitation and a delight to be part of the journey. When traditional leadership hits the millennial, an epidemic of disengagement is generated. Today, we need to move our leadership thinking and practices to the next level - Mindful Leadership.

Mindful Leadership demands that we move away from a reductionist view, pegging leadership effectiveness to a single silver bullet whether it is drive, passion, innovation, visionary, results driven etc. Folkman and Zenger talk about combining strengths into clusters or companion skills that work in symphony. Powerful combinations like quality focus, right direction and speed lead to innovation and enhanced performance. Such strength combinations, in my opinion, augurs well for leadership effectiveness today. Imagine the outcomes associated with quality focus, wrong priorities and speed.

Adams and Anderson of the Full Circle Group, deepen the leadership conversation by focusing on mastering leadership. They looked at non-differentiating strengths and found that a number of universalistic qualities, while necessary, do not impact significantly. Hard-working, continuous improvement, domain knowledge, results focus - they all fall in this category. Adams and Anderson also look at the cancelling effect where certain liabilities and derailers offset the strengths of leaders. As such, drive and passion, visionary skills and even results focus, can be compromised or diminished by weak people skills, lack of team building and listening skills. In short, they were confirming the relevance of the Peter Principle (what got us here will not take us there). More important today, is a recognition that how we get results, is as important as the results themselves. We need to guard against those instinctive biases leading to ineffective interaction styles, team under-development, micromanaging, over-demanding and self-centricity. Instead, energy must be invested in strengthening the cluster of strong people skills, visionary team leadership, team building and good listening. In other words, leadership orientation, specifically Mindful Leadership, must be included in PG's lessons. This goes beyond ambition, controller and driver, allowing us to maximize strengths without letting our liabilities and derailers hijack us.

F. CONCLUSION

Abraham Lincoln said "nearly all great men can stand adversity, but if you want to test a man's character, give him power." With PG, we may be dealing with a man who, at the core, is first a philosopher and upon whom, corporate responsibilities were assigned. He could not have defected from this task given his nationalistic inclination. He pursued his mission as artists do, with a passion, confidence and self-centricity fashioning managerial and leadership behaviors here and there intentionally and serendipitously.

Interestingly, Naipaul does not only see us as "mimic men". He would have us believe, "The world is what it is, men who are nothing, who allow themselves to become nothing, have no place in it..." To this I can state categorically, Not PG. He was a man on a mission with a story to tell. In a way doing his own performance assessment - the other reviews having been done on him over the last 2 decades. As leader, he has held the management principle of responsibility with accountability in high esteem.

Times of national resistance in the '70s, accompanied by the call to design a better place for all of us to inhabit, caused this man to change his personal plans. NCB - Nationals Conquering Banking - was an assignment, given his early conditioning of family, school and church, that he could not defect from. He accepted the assignment and had the courage to empower his charges to take action - a privilege that very few bankers at the local level, enjoyed then, and even now. Decision-making at the highest level of corporate operations, done on local soil - this will remain one of the true legacies of PG's NCB.

His final chapter, "Your life's joyous expansion" shows up this philosopher / artist of the corporate type. An intuitive and personal communicator, he paints the big picture, avoiding details with a nuanced connection and feel, not sufficiently appreciating those among us who were analytical and functional, and needed data, evidence, numbers, details or timelines. Probably there were times when he could have stopped members of his senior team from falling into the trap of exchanging smart sounding ideas and constructs, instead of making measurable forward progress... just talking about the situation like "problem admirers". He could have encouraged more strategic action. But this required listening of a different order.

Some would have us believe in the concept of co-leadership and reverse mentoring, and researcher A Fiedler takes it further by introducing the possibility of automating management. While that may be so, leadership will always be paramount, especially in these parts where the role and process of social capital formation is not fully appreciated and remains a mystery even in the boardroom.

As good students do, they leave their last words to the teacher. In the conclusion of his book, PG asks, "What is the purpose of one's journey in entering this world?". He answers later on, "...the point is that I followed my dreams" and further reminds us, "You can excel and leave your unique legacy." Thanks PG for this reflective personal account of your stewardship. Job well done.

Front Cover of my previous book published by Balboa Press entitled "Think, Be Still, & Grow Spiritually."

Back cover of the book "Think, Be Still, & Grow Spiritually"
By Philip Guy Rochford

The framework

The journey of spirituality is unique to each individual, therefore, you need a compass. And the message in Think, Be Still, & Grow Spiritually can be used to form a useful spiritual framework. The title reflects the fact that thinking is a pre-condition to manifest anything, but that thinking has to be properly channeled.

The spiritual framework is explained using the acronym FOLDING, for forgiveness, openness, learning, denial, intentionality, nurturing, and gratitude. These elements are separated for purposes of illustration, although they are all interconnected.

Think, Be Still, & Grow Spiritually shows:

- the nature and scope of the declarations that are at the heart of spiritual development
- how spiritual and physical bodies work with each other
- how essential universal laws have an impact on your daily living
- what constitutes your spiritual manifesto

READ THE RANGE OF REVIEWS AT THE FRONT OF THE BOOK TO GAIN FURTHER INSIGHTS.

Front cover of my last book published by Balboa Press entitled "10 Proven 21st Century Success Generators."

SELF IMPROVEMENT

Philip Guy Rochford in his careers of economist, banker, consultant, author, and life coach has used 10 Proven Success Generators herein to produce highly successful results for himself, and many thousands of other persons.

He has 5 children alive, married to Edlin, herself an author, and they live in Trinidad.

The Power Plant does not have energy, it GENERATES energy. Similarly, persons do not have energy they generate energy. You therefore need a framework to assist your generation of energy. The Ten Success Generators outlined in "10 Proven 21st Century Success Generators" set the boundaries for generating your success. The generators are: Desire • Health • Belief • Action • Standards • Habits • Contribution • Knowledge • Creativity • Intentionality.

There are different platforms to deliver successful life results, but these 10 Success Generators provide a useful proven framework to deliver high performance results.

The content of "10 Proven 21st Century Success Generators" show:

- The knowledge, wisdom and understanding underlying each Success Generator.
- The boundaries of the main concepts relative to individual Success Generators.
- The most important points derived from the concepts of each Success Generator.
- How to pursue a different routine for each Success Generator in order to improve or deepen the particular Success Generator.

You can claim the life you want, if you put your attention on your intention, and deliver massive action consistent with the vision you have for your life. You can do it. It's possible!

After re-visiting what you already know of the Ten Success Generators, you are invited to make your Common Knowledge become Common Practice. What's your next bold move to take you to your next higher step of success? Act now and start moving to your next higher level of success.

U.S. $15.99

ISBN 976-1-5043-5872-9
51599

BALBOA

9 781504 358729

PHILIP GUY ROCHFORD

10 Proven 21st Century Success Generators

Guaranteed to provide you with better success results

Foreword by **Dr. Theodore U. Ferguson**,
Educator & Author of "Writings on
Leadership: Sharing the Philosophy of Leading
From Above The Line"

10 Proven 21st Century Success Generators

PHILIP GUY ROCHFORD

BACK COVER *(My last book published by Balboa Press entitled "10 Proven 21ˢᵗ Century Success Generators.")*

The Power Plant does not have energy, it GENERATES energy. Similarly, persons do not have energy they generate energy. You therefore need a framework to assist your generation of energy. The Ten Success Generators outlined in "10 Proven *21ˢᵗ Century* Success Generators" set the boundaries for generating your success. The generators are: Desire ⬌ Health ⬌ Belief ⬌ Action ⬌ Standards ⬌ Habits ⬌ Contribution ⬌ Knowledge ⬌ Creativity ⬌ Intentionality.

There are different platforms to deliver successful life results, but these 10 Success Generators provide a useful proven framework to deliver high performance results.

The content of "10 Proven *21ˢᵗ Century* Success Generators" show:

- The knowledge, wisdom and understanding underlying each Success Generator.
- The boundaries of the main concepts relative to individual Success Generators.
- The most important points derived from the concepts of each Success Generator.
- How to pursue a different routine for each Success Generator in order to improve or deepen the particular Success Generator.

You can claim the life you want, if you put your attention on your intention, and deliver massive action consistent with the vision you have for your life. You can do it. It's possible!

After re-visiting what you already know of the Ten Success Generators, you are invited to make your Common Knowledge become Common Practice. What's your next bold move to take you to your next higher step of success? Act now and start moving to your next higher level of success.

INDEX

222